D1474081

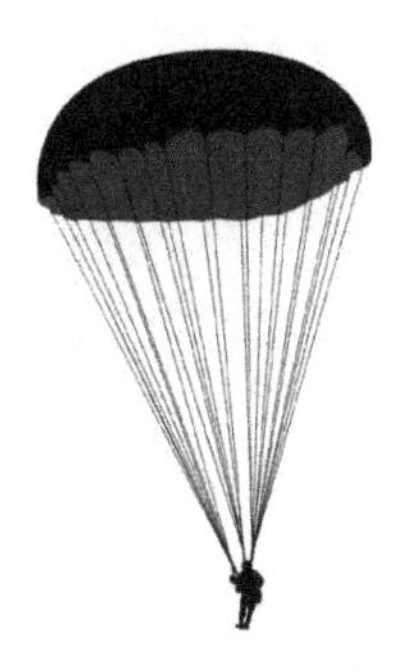

GROW YOUR GRIT

Overcome Obstacles, Thrive, and Accomplish Your Goals

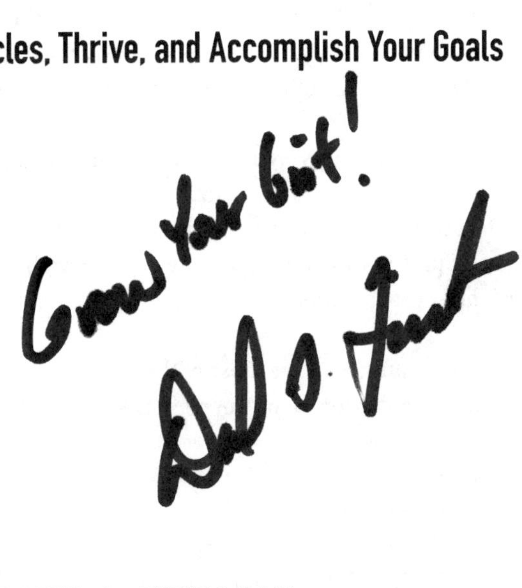

DAVID G. FIVECOAT

TFCG

Grow Your Grit
Overcome Obstacles, Thrive, and Accomplish Your Goals

ISBNs:
978-1-7368933-0-2 (paperback)
978-1-7368933-1-9 (hardcover)
978-1-7368933-2-6 (eBook)

Published by:
TFCG, LLC
604 Broadway
Columbus, Georgia 31901

Advanced Praise for *Grow Your Grit*

"*Grow Your Grit* provides a clear and compelling blueprint for a critical task—developing individual grit, that all-important leadership quality of sheer determination that enables us to overcome obstacles, drive on in the face of adversity, and persevere through hardship. David Fivecoat—with whom I was privileged to serve several tours in Iraq and Afghanistan—leverages his enormous experience and considerable expertise from leading Army units through years of tough combat and also in significant peacetime tasks to provide a book that is a must-read for any leader at any level seeking to build fortitude and grit!"

General David Petraeus, US Army, Retired,
former commander of the surge in Iraq
and former director of the CIA

"A fantastic read from someone who knows a thing or two about grit, and a must-read for anyone looking to better understand what it takes to achieve the seemingly impossible. *Grow Your Grit* brings to life just how individuals and organizations achieve success amid adversity through multifaceted, real-life examples. Most important, *Grow Your Grit* empowers readers to work toward sharpening their own grit by providing roadmaps and resources to do just that."

Anna Zaccaria,
US Army officer and analyst at Deloitte

"Fivecoat's *Grit* framework is a solid tool for any leader, current or aspiring!"

Josh Powers,
founder of the Field Grade Leader website

"Major Dick Winters and Easy Company, 506th Parachute Infantry Regiment had grit in spades. David Fivecoat captures how to create similar grit in your organization."

Colonel Cole Kingseed, US Army, Retired,
NY Times Best Selling Author of *Beyond Band of Brothers*

"Grit powered West Point's basketball team to an undefeated season in 1944 – and victory on the battlefields beyond. *Grow Your Grit* provides a blueprint for you to develop the same grit within your business and dominate the competition.»

Jim Noles,
Author of *Undefeated: From Basketball to Battle – West Point's Perfect 1944 Season*

For my daughter, Nora,
my inspiration
to be the grittiest leader I can possibly be
and help others be the best that they can be.

ACKNOWLEDGMENTS

Putting a book together requires a great deal of organization, discipline, patience, and teamwork. This book is no exception to that rule. First, I'd like to thank Suzanne Williams for providing the catalyst for me to write the book. It was a great idea!

I'd also like to thank Nora Fivecoat, Terrance Avery, Anna Zaccaria, Josh Powers, Margaret Morris, Jennifer Chan, and Larry Glasscock for all your efforts reading and providing feedback on early versions of *Grow Your Grit*. You really helped improve the book.

Kimberly Martin and her entire team at Jera Publishing were amazing with their efforts to bring this book to the marketplace. Kimberly mentored me every step of the way. Jason Orr did a phenomenal job with the cover. I can't recommend Jera Publishing highly enough.

Finally, my editor was amazing! Over the course of two months, Candace Johnson took a good book and turned it into a great book with her incredible editing skills. Her team at Change It Up Editing and Writing Services is topnotch.

CONTENTS

INTRODUCTION

SHARANA, PAKTIKA PROVINCE, AFGHANISTAN, AUGUST 2010

I WAS SITTING IN A large, faux-marble room on the second floor of the Governor's Palace in Paktika Province. As a thirty-nine-year-old battalion commander, I was on my fourth combat tour and now leading the 600 soldiers in the Iron Rakkasans (3rd Battalion, 187 Infantry) strung out in small bases across the hot, high-desert plain. After almost 1,000 days in combat in Iraq and Afghanistan, I was on the road six days a week, dodging improvised explosive devices, bullets, and rocket-propelled grenades (RPGs), to see my soldiers and work with our Afghan partners.

As the fan moved lazily on the ceiling, I was doing my best to stay engaged in yet another meeting with the provincial governor, the provincial police chief, the Afghanistan National Army Brigade commander, and the chief of the National Directorate of Security (NDS—the domestic and foreign intelligence agency of Afghanistan) for Paktika.

The meeting ground to a halt as the police chief started yelling at Lieutenant Colonel Mir Wais, the Afghan Army Brigade Commander, for not following up on some information. In one of the couches next to the governor, the NDS chief took a phone call. After hanging up, the NDS chief stopped the meeting and said he had intelligence on rockets pointed at Forward Operating Base (FOB) Sharana, a sprawling US base with thousands of soldiers and contractors on the outskirts of the city. More importantly to me, FOB Sharana was home to 200 of my soldiers.

The four Afghan leaders bickered about whose responsibility it was to go find the rockets. My interpreter tried to keep up with the conversation, but it was clear that no one was going to do anything about it. Finally, I had had enough—through my interpreter I called out the police, the army, and the NDS.

I said, "Each of you be on the street outside the compound in fifteen minutes with a platoon of people [about thirty]. We will *all* go get the rockets. Anybody who doesn't show up will no longer receive our assistance and training." That ended the debate as each leader scrambled to find their men.

I called my guys on the radio and told them to get ready. The governor and I chatted for a couple of minutes, and then I went down to the street. My threat had worked—there was a huge convoy of Afghan Army soldiers, Afghan policemen, and NDS already milling about our four Mine-Resistant Ambush Protected (MRAPs) vehicles. These sixteen-ton armored trucks were designed to redirect the blast from an IED to protect the crew, but they weren't very nimble off-road.

The NDS chief and I talked for a second—he had gotten another call that the rockets were in a "garden" southeast of the FOB. "Garden" could mean anything in the translation from Pashto to English—some woods, a field, a grape arbor, or a grove. We decided to split the force and have half come from the east and half come from the west. The NDS chief and I decided to go to the west.

We drove to the traffic circle and headed south on Route Audi toward the small village of Yosef Khel. My detachment leader, Staff

Sergeant Padilla, decided to follow a dirt road, but it rapidly disappeared. We stopped and left the two MRAP trucks and crews in defensive positions before they got stuck in the soft soil. My truck and Sergeant Grawzis's MRAP continued to chase the NDS's Toyota pickup trucks across the desert.

The NDS chief stopped near a grove of trees, got out, and questioned a couple of farmers. They hadn't seen anything, but he was able to climb up on the roof of a *qalat* (a mud-brick walled compound) and make a cell phone call. Evidently his source was near because he climbed down, jumped back in the truck, and took off for another grove of trees farther east. We followed, bumping across the desert at thirty miles per hour.

Three (of the Five) Rockets Pointed at FOB Sharana

The convoy of Afghan and American troops maneuvered around some *qalats* and found another orchard. Approaching cautiously, we spotted five 107 mm rockets on rails pointed northwest at FOB

Sharana. The 107 mm rockets could have been built by the Russians, the Chinese, or the Iranians, but regardless of their builder, they pack a punch—after flying seven miles, their warhead flings shrapnel fifty meters. All the rockets were linked to a timer that was counting down the minutes until launch. Tick. Tick. Tick. I used the radio to call for an explosive ordnance disposal (EOD) team to help us, but it was going to take them over an hour to arrive. Time was slipping away from us. We had to try something else.

Grawzis, the NDS chief, and I discussed trying to hook them with a rope and pull them over, but we weren't sure if they were booby-trapped. After we walked around the rockets, we discarded that idea. I decided to bring in Apache attack helicopters to destroy them.

I called the nearby helicopter battalion, Task Force Gambler, and in a few minutes the Apaches arrived overhead with their distinctive thwock-thwock. After helping the pilots see the Taliban rockets, the pair of helicopters took turns shooting them with Hellfire missiles, 2.75" rockets, and gun runs. After each attack, I (or one of the soldiers) would walk forward, check to see if the rockets were disabled, and then order another gun run. On the fourth gun run, one of the Taliban rockets detonated and went whizzing across the field where it exploded harmlessly. The last of the five got knocked over. Relief! The FOB and its thousands of people were safe from the threat.

The EOD team arrived an hour later and destroyed the remnants of the rockets. Our Afghan partners and my team returned to our bases; we were proud we had made Paktika Province a little safer that day. It was a small step to get everyone to work together to solve the crisis, even if it took a threat.

I was on my thirty-sixth month of combat in Iraq and Afghanistan. I had gotten up every day for a thousand days. I had risked life and limb. Counterinsurgency is a Sisyphean task. Why didn't I let the Afghan military deal with the rockets? Why did I feel the need to personally go after the rockets?

One of the main reasons I went after the rockets was my grit.

THE GRIT PROJECT

Ten years later, my grit project started in the fall of 2020 when a friend asked me to take a look at some material on grit. Several years earlier I had enjoyed reading Angela Duckworth's *Grit: The Power of Passion and Perseverance.* As I read the material, I realized that it, like Duckworth's book, fell short on telling me how to build my own grit and the grit of teams I was leading.

Tenacity. Persistence. Perseverance. Determination. Work ethic. Relentlessness. Fortitude. Toughness. Resolve. Endurance. These are just a few of the words that describe people and organizations who overcome obstacles to achieve long-term goals. But not everyone or every group has it. It isn't easy to acquire. But whatever its name is, grit exists as a behavior in both people and groups.

My own experience with grit started early. I grew up in Delaware, Ohio, a small town in the middle of the state. My father grew up on a farm in eastern Ohio and was the first in his family to graduate from college. He was extremely hardworking around the house, at his job, and as a coach. He taught me the value of a strong work ethic through his personal example and the legendary stories of his father's hard work on the farm, in the sawmill, and in the coal mines. From this foundation, I developed my own grit through a series of gritty journeys where I earned my Eagle Scout badge, graduated from West Point, earned the Ranger Tab from the US Army's Ranger School, led soldiers during four combat deployments, raced in triathlons, and established a small business during the pandemic.

As I reflected more, I realized that I had quite a bit of experience with grit. Over the years I had developed some of my own thoughts on how to build grit in myself, in another person, and in an organization. Grit has powered me to train to race Ironman 70.3s, earn two master's degrees, and recover from a fractured scapula. It has powered organizations I was part of from the Delaware Hayes High School football team on the gridiron to the Iron Rakkasans in Afghanistan and my consulting company during the pandemic. I realized some of my ideas and experiences might be able to help others and other organizations grow their grit, so I decided that I would test drive them in my blog. Surprisingly, the posts were a hit—thousands of people read the articles and wanted to talk and learn about growing their grit.

THE BOOK

Writing a book takes grit, too. With the success of the blog, it became apparent that a book was the best way to reach a wider audience and help more people. Through a quarantine, the holidays, and the cold winter weather, I wrote day in and day out, reviewed, revised, and wrote some more.

Personal grit and organizational grit are similar, yet different. I believe that personal grit is the will to persevere to achieve long-term goals. And I believe that a person's grit is built upon six components: a purpose, a goal, their perseverance, their resilience, their courage to deal with the fear of failure, and their motivation. The first section of the book covers personal grit and each of the six components. Stories of Ulysses Grant, John Rockefeller, Sara Blakely, Dan Gable, Misty Copeland, Amelia Earhart, Michael Jordan, Ruth Bader Ginsberg, Mia Hamm, and a few of my own help provide insight.

The second section concentrates on organizational grit. My definition of organizational grit is "the group's will to persevere to achieve long-term goals," and it is developed by providing the team a purpose, a goal and a plan, a scoreboard, a gritty culture, and by building trust in the team. Most importantly, though, this process of creating a gritty organization requires strong leadership. Along the way, the book uses multiple concepts to examine and explain grit. The military tools of Leader's Intent, a planning process, the Operations Order, and the After Action Review are offered as ways to provide a group a purpose, a plan, and an inclusive way to learn from its experiences. The culture of the National Aeronautics and Space Administration (NASA) during the Apollo program is an example of a large organization that aligned its purpose and values to create a team that achieved extraordinary results. And Currahee Mountain, the crucible that forged the team that became the Band of Brothers, makes the case for each part of organizational grit.

Growing grit is not an easy journey. Processes and systems help make the journey more manageable. In each section, I break down grit into its parts, determine ways to optimize each part, and encourage and inspire you to apply the ideas to grow your personal grit and your organization's grit. Each chapter uses stories from the military, business, and athletics to reinforce the lesson. For personal grit, I put it all back together with a checklist in Chapter 10 for you to utilize as you work toward growing your grit. For organizational grit, I provide a summary and give you a strategy to follow with your organization with the blueprint in Chapter 18.

For the readers who believe they already have exceptional grit, I ask that you read the book from start to finish. For the readers who believe they need to grow their grit, pick a chapter or two where you think you really need help and focus your efforts there. Wherever you are in your personal grit journey, and wherever your team is with its journey toward organizational grit, the book has something for you. Whatever way you choose to use the book, it will help you better understand grit, break it down into manageable parts, show you ways to optimize it, and grow your grit.

The grit to persevere daily in combat and disrupt a rocket attack took me years to develop. Growing grit isn't always easy or quick. It isn't always simple. But it is possible if you understand how it works.

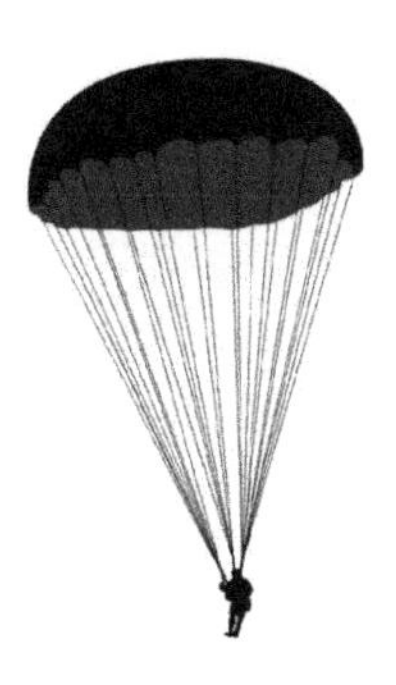

SECTION I:

GROW YOUR PERSONAL GRIT

Chapter 1

PERSONAL GRIT

At midnight after almost being defeated on the first day during the Battle of Shiloh in the American Civil War, General William T. Sherman found his boss, General Ulysses S. Grant, huddled under a tree in a driving rainstorm, smoking a cigar. Sherman approached the tree and said, "Well, Grant, we've had the devil's own day, haven't we?"

"Yep. Lick 'em tomorrow, though," replied General Ulysses S. Grant.

THE FIRST DAY OF THE BATTLE OF SHILOH was not General Ulysses S. Grant's finest hour. Surprised by a smaller Confederate army, outflanked and outfought, the Union army was almost driven into the Tennessee River. Despite these obstacles, Grant inspired his men with his dogged determination and grit. After more troops arrived when the sun went down, General Grant launched a counterattack in the early morning hours of April 7, 1862, snatched victory from the jaws of defeat, and forced the Confederate army to retreat. After tenaciously achieving victories at the battles of Vicksburg and Chattanooga, President Abraham Lincoln promoted Grant to command all the

Union Armies in 1864. From this position, Grant orchestrated the defeat of the Confederate States of America by putting pressure on the rebels from five directions simultaneously.

Grant didn't find his personal grit at midnight in a rainstorm on a battlefield; he had been practicing and growing personal grit his entire life. Growing up the son of a tanner in Ohio, he learned the value of hard work at a young age. While at the United States Military Academy at West Point, he was selected as the most proficient horseman in his class; he also read widely and graduated twenty-first overall. During the Mexican-American War from 1846 to 1848, Grant deployed with the US Army to invade Mexico. He demonstrated bravery, courage, and grit in multiple battles, earning the respect of his peers. Despite the grit he displayed in combat in Mexico, Grant's grit and resiliency were tested after the war—he failed as a peacetime soldier, failed as a farmer, failed as a woodcutter, and failed as a bill collector. Despite these failures, each time he managed to rebound, dust himself off, and start on a new path.

Starting off the war as a colonel in the Illinois volunteers, Grant rose rapidly through the ranks, eventually becoming a lieutenant general. As Lincoln said of him, "I can't spare this man, he fights." As the architect of the United States' strategy, Grant's grit was the catalyst for the Union victory during the Civil War.

Post-war, he leveraged his notoriety all the way to the presidency. After two terms in the White House, Grant continued to exhibit grit. He worked as an executive for the Mexican Southern Railroad, which eventually went bankrupt. Afterward, he became a partner in the Grant & Ward brokerage house. It, too, went bankrupt due to a series of fraudulent investments by his partner, Ferdinand Ward.

A few months after the failure of Grant & Ward, Grant was diagnosed with cancer. With his back against the wall and his family facing bankruptcy, he agreed to write his autobiography in exchange for an unheard-of 70 percent royalty. Always a good storyteller and writer, Grant finished his *Personal Memoirs of U. S. Grant* four days before he died. The book was a commercial success—his wife received today's equivalent of $12.8 million from its sales. Even today, the book is considered to be the best autobiography of any American general.

Grant's grit, tenacity, and resilience enabled him to keep putting one foot in front of the other to overcome obstacles in Mexico, in a series of failed jobs between the wars, challenges during the Civil War, trials during his presidency, and a series of failed executive positions after the White House. Grit turned the son of an Ohio tanner into an extraordinary figure in the nineteenth century.

PERSONAL GRIT

A recent study found that 92 percent of people that set New Year's goals never actually achieve them. But why do the 8 percent succeed and accomplish their goals? I think it is because this small group practiced effective goal setting, persevered, had the resilience to overcome setbacks, possessed the courage to deal with the fear of failure, and maintained their motivation to succeed. In a word, they had grit.

Grit is an intangible trait that helps people accomplish extraordinary goals. Grit is that thing that gets you to study for one more test as you earn your degree, swim one more lap in the pool to get ready for the state championship, or skip the daily cappuccino to save for a trip to Europe. Grit can help take your leadership, fitness, relationships, education, and teams to the next level. High-performing students, parents, leaders, entrepreneurs, and athletes are using grit right now to achieve their long-term goals.

Angela Duckworth, a professor of psychology at the University of Pennsylvania, brought grit to the forefront through her TED Talk, numerous articles, and the 2016 book *Grit: The Power of Passion and Perseverance.* Through years of research, Duckworth defines grit as the "combination of passion and perseverance that made high achievers special." Duckworth further breaks individual grit down as a combination of interest (enjoyment), practice (a persistent desire to do better), purpose (their personal *why*), and hope (the ability to bounce back).

Grit has been compared to conscientiousness, one of the Big Five personality traits. The Big Five are a group of five broad dimensions that psychologists use to describe the human personality and psyche: openness to experience, conscientiousness, extraversion, agreeableness, and neuroticism. Grit is most associated with conscientiousness, which is described as the tendency to be responsible, organized, hard-working, goal-directed, and to adhere to norms and rules. However, conscientiousness lacks the long-term aspect of grit. Since Duckworth's book was published, psychologists have argued whether grit exists, how different it is from conscientiousness, and how different it is from perseverance.

I find Duckworth's book compelling. She does a phenomenal job describing what grit is and how you can determine your level of grit. Like Duckworth, I believe grit exists and can be grown. Nevertheless, I think she falls short when providing practical ways to grow your grit or your organization's grit. I also diverge from Duckworth in that I don't believe that grit requires passion. Some things I do daily are gritty but aren't fueled by a particular passion. For instance, I foam roll and stretch after every workout. I don't have a particular passion for it, but it feels good, has helped me stay flexible and recover from tough workouts, and benefits my long-term goal of being an athlete.

GRIT REDUX

I'm not a psychologist like Duckworth and her peers. Rather, I am a practitioner of grit. From becoming an Eagle Scout to graduating from the United States Military Academy at West Point, from earning the Ranger Tab from the US Army's Ranger School to completing multiple combat deployments in Iraq and Afghanistan, from training and competing in triathlons to starting a business in the midst of the pandemic, I am no stranger to gritty journeys, both successful and learning experiences. These crucibles and others have forged my grit. And I continue to find value in finding gritty journeys to pursue, grow, and develop.

My experience with grit has led me to believe that in contrast to Duckworth's definition, grit is better defined as "the will to persevere to achieve long-term goals." Furthermore, I believe a person's grit is built upon six components: purpose, goal, perseverance, resilience, courage to deal with the fear of failure, and motivation. These components can be further broken down.

- Purpose is your personal *why*.
- Goal is a desired outcome in the future.
- Perseverance is persistence in doing something difficult.
- Resilience is the capacity to recover from difficulties or toughness.
- Courage is the management of the fear of failure.
- Motivation is the fuel that feeds the grit fire.

When we bring these six elements together, we create grit. Grit helps people and organizations accomplish extraordinary tasks.

What is Personal Grit?

The will to persevere to achieve long term goals

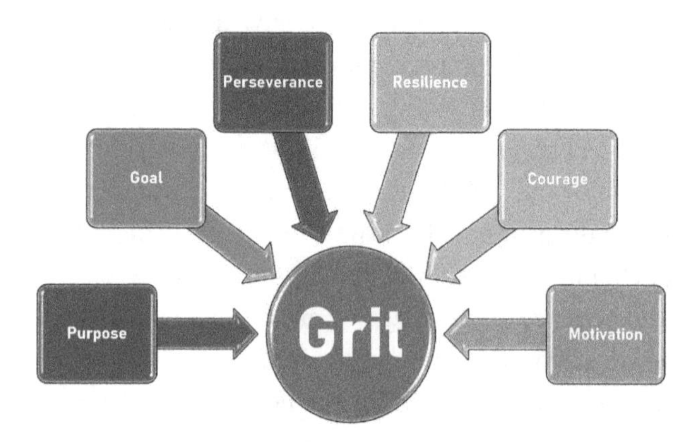

Personal Grit

Grit is built upon the mundane—making hundreds and hundreds of incremental improvements across the six components. The key to growing your grit is in making incremental improvements in each of these components over the course of weeks, months, and years: your goal setting, perseverance, resilience, courage to deal with the fear of failure, and motivation. Doing a series of little things right, day in and day out, is the key to growing your grit.

The beauty of grit is that you don't have to be born with it. Gritty people are made. Grit is acquired through experiences, self-development, training, observation, and exposure to other gritty people. Now, that's not to say it's easy, but fortunately, people can be trained to be gritty and can transfer grit developed in one arena to another. For example, walking 10,000 steps every day for a month may give you enough grit to tackle a particularly challenging long-term project at work. Or finally finish that lingering project in your yard.

THE SCIENCE BEHIND GRIT

Kelly McGonigal, PhD, is a psychology instructor at Stanford and the author of *The Willpower Instinct: How Self-Control Works*. The book is a great guide to increasing your willpower. I have adapted some of her thoughts on the brain, physiology, and muscles to my ideas on grit.

The Brain

The human brain is an amazing organ and a key factor in growing grit. The prefrontal cortex, which comprises 12 percent of the average three-pound brain, is the bedrock of your personal grit. Located directly behind the forehead, the prefrontal cortex plays a role in planning complex cognitive behavior, personality expression, moderating social behavior, and moderating certain aspects of speech and language. More importantly, the prefrontal cortex orchestrates thoughts and actions to accomplish goals, which, of course, is a critical component of grit.

Another important function of the brain involved with grit is the neurotransmitter called *dopamine*. When the brain recognizes an opportunity for a reward, like eating candy, it releases a dopamine, and that dopamine tells the rest of the brain to act to get the reward. When released, the dopamine causes a feeling of alertness and arousal—it is a feeling of anticipation of happiness. If you can link your dopamine release to achieving gritty goals or positive habits, you can create an exceptionally powerful tool.

Finally, the brain helps us exercise self-control in the pursuit of long-term goals. Many people believe that being tough on themselves is the only way to accomplish anything. Interestingly, research shows that self-criticism is consistently associated with decreased motivation and poor self-control. Instead, supportive, compassionate self-talk such as forgiveness and encouragement tend to result in better motivation because it boosts personal responsibility and learning.

Physiology

Grit also has biological characteristics. When you need to exercise grit, your brain and body set a chain of activities in motion that help you make a tough decision or resist temptation. Suzanne Sagerstrom, a psychologist at the University of Kentucky, has termed this the *pause-and-plan response*. You can think of it as the opposite of the more well-known *fight-or-flight response*.

When your mind recognizes a threat to a long-term goal, it tries to help you make the right choice by invoking the pause-and-plan response. First, the prefrontal cortex tells your body to send energy to the brain to make the necessary decision. Second, it puts the body into a calmer state by slowing the heart rate, maintaining blood pressure levels, and slowing your breathing, which relaxes the body and puts the mind into a state to make a decision. Conversely, we have the fight-or-flight response that activates the autonomic nervous system causing a quickened pulse, dilated pupils, dry mouth, and increased breathing to manage stress.

To identify how well your body is dealing with stress, measure the time between heartbeats, your Heart Rate Variability (HRV). The more variability, or difference in time between beats, the better your body is dealing with stress. Higher HRV is also a key indicator of better willpower and grit. The Whoop, Oura Ring, Apple Watch, and Garmin Watches all provide you the ability to track aspects of your HRV.

Once you are tracking your HRV, you will see trends over time as your HRV goes up and down. Fortunately, sleep, recovery from tough workouts, good nutrition, eliminating alcohol, and mindfulness can help increase your HRV, your physical performance, your ability to deal with stress, and your grit.

The pause-and-plan response is more subtle than the flight-or-fight response. Nevertheless, your brain and body work together to help you make tough decisions. It isn't always enough to resist eating that cookie and breaking your diet, but it helps.

Grit Muscle

Muscles are amazing. You go to the gym and deadlift. The muscle breaks down, responds to the stimulus, and grows. Do too many deadlifts and your core will be tired and sore for several days. Skip three weeks at the gym and you won't be able to lift the same amount you did the last time you worked out.

Grit is, in many ways, like a muscle. At the beginning of the day, your grit is strong. Use it to make decisions or make progress toward a gritty goal and it tires, gradually losing its ability to help you make tough decisions. Get a good night's sleep and your grit will bounce back the next day. In light of this, it may be helpful to schedule tough decisions in the morning when your grit is close to full strength.

Fortunately, the grit muscle can be trained, and the development is transferable to other gritty tasks. Small, consistent, gritty acts like avoiding sweets, balancing your checkbook every month, flossing your teeth every night, and writing a to-do list every day can increase your overall grit. Although these small gritty activities seem insignificant, they contribute to increasing grit for the areas that are more important to you. Be on the lookout for small, gritty tasks to add to your daily routine to help grow your grit muscle.

GRITTY JOURNEY

You might achieve a better understanding of grit by taking you through my own personal gritty journey from this past year. Zwift is a game that enables you to link your smart power bicycle trainer or treadmill to your computer, enabling you to ride with other cyclists or run with other runners in a virtual environment. Beyond the collaboration aspect, the virtual environment enables you to earn badges, compete against other users, or follow specific training sessions designed by professional coaches. More importantly, through its gamification of the workout, Zwift helps to relieve some of the boredom associated with indoor riding or running.

For the cyclist, Zwift awards badges every time you complete a new route or a significant accomplishment. Late last summer, an old boss and one-time running partner casually asked me how many badges I had earned because he had just earned his one hundredth badge. I had been using Zwift for the past four years but hadn't paid much attention to the badges. I checked and discovered that I had only fifty-nine badges. Darn! I knew it was time to get gritty.

So, I developed my gritty goal: earn 100 badges before January 1, 2021. To help my perseverance, I broke the goal down by listing all the routes and accomplishments available to me to get the forty-one badges I needed. I eliminated some, like the London's PRL Full Badge, a ride that would take seven-plus hours on the bike to ride its 107 virtual miles. Instead, I focused on forty-one badges that I could achieve with my daily workout. I built my resilience by talking regularly to a cycling friend about the gritty journey. I enhanced my courage by accepting that during some workouts I would run out of time to earn the badge and I would merely have a learning experience. I fueled my motivation by checking the scoreboard after every workout and by telling others about the journey and talking trash to the friend with 100 badges.

Even with all that, the gritty journey to get 100 badges took me until December 24, when I received my 100th badge for doing the "Serpentine 8" route.

GRIT BASELINE

Before you start on improving your grit or you begin a gritty journey, it is worthwhile to take a baseline assessment of how gritty you are currently. There are dozens of grit quizzes online, but to make your life a little easier, I included one below. It is important to take the time to figure out what your starting point looks like, especially since grit involves the progression towards the achievement of a long-term goal.

The questions in this quiz focus on moments you demonstrated grit in the last year. It may help to compare yourself to the average American as you work your way through the quiz. In 2018, the average American was a non-Hispanic white woman who was fifty-two years-old. The average American had a bachelor's degree, worked in education and health services, earned $889 per week, and lived in a house in a city.

There is also an online version of the quiz at my website—www.thefivecoatconsultinggroup.com. Take the quiz and see how gritty you are.

GRIT QUIZ

1. How often do you work hard at a task?
   - ☐ Always
   - ☐ Usually
   - ☐ About half the time
   - ☐ Seldom
   - ☐ Never

2. Do you enjoy working on challenging projects?
    - ☐ Always
    - ☐ Usually
    - ☐ About half the time
    - ☐ Seldom
    - ☐ Never
3. Over the past twelve months, were you able to accomplish all your long-range goals?
    - ☐ Always
    - ☐ Usually
    - ☐ About half the time
    - ☐ Seldom
    - ☐ Never
4. Do you use past mistakes to help you solve current problems?
    - ☐ Always
    - ☐ Usually
    - ☐ About half the time
    - ☐ Seldom
    - ☐ Never
5. Over the past twelve months, did you bounce back quickly from failure or negative feedback?
    - ☐ Always
    - ☐ Usually
    - ☐ About half the time
    - ☐ Seldom
    - ☐ Never
6. Over the past twelve months, how often did you complete everything you began?
    - ☐ Always
    - ☐ Usually
    - ☐ About half the time
    - ☐ Seldom
    - ☐ Never
7. Do you tell others about your goals even if there is a possibility of failure?
    - ☐ Always
    - ☐ Usually
    - ☐ About half the time

- ☐ Seldom
- ☐ Never

8. Do you write down and track personal and professional goals?
   - ☐ Always
   - ☐ Usually
   - ☐ About half the time
   - ☐ Seldom
   - ☐ Never
9. Over the last twelve months, how often did you overcome significant obstacles to accomplish a goal?
   - ☐ Always
   - ☐ Usually
   - ☐ About half the time
   - ☐ Seldom
   - ☐ Never
10. Do you set professional goals beyond your current role?
    - ☐ Always
    - ☐ Usually
    - ☐ About half the time
    - ☐ Seldom
    - ☐ Never

Give yourself 5 points for every Always, 4 points for every Usually, 3 Points for every About half the time, 2 Points for every Seldom, and 1 Point for every Never.

Total your points up, and here is where you stand.

- Highly Gritty: 40–50
- Average Grit: 20–39
- Low Grit: 0–19

Now that you know where you are, you can start developing your grit little-by-little.

CONCLUSION

Ulysses S. Grant's grit propelled him from Point Pleasant, Ohio to General of the Union Armies and architect of the defeat of the Confederate States of America. It fueled his work as a two-term United States president, but more importantly, it helped him overcome a series of setbacks in jobs spanning more than a decade between the wars and as an executive in two companies after the White House. The grit, persistence, ability to bounce back from disaster after disaster, and the courage to deal with the fear of failure that Grant exhibited during his life, are remarkable. He is in the top 1 percent of all gritty individuals.

Grit is intangible but incredibly powerful. Your personal grit, like Grant's, is built upon your purpose, your goal, your perseverance, your resilience to deal with setbacks, your courage to deal with the fear of failure, and your motivation. Understanding each part of it will help you leverage your strengths and improve your shortcomings as you grow your grit.

Now, you probably aren't trying to win the Civil War or even earn a hundred badges on Zwift, but going on the offensive and growing your grit can make you more successful as a person, a parent, and a leader. Find your gritty goal and begin building your perseverance, resilience, courage, and motivation to accomplish it.

Chapter 2

FIND YOUR PERSONAL PURPOSE

"Singleness of purpose is one of the chief essentials for success in life, no matter what may be one's aim."

John D. Rockefeller, Sr., founder and CEO, Standard Oil Company

JOHN D. ROCKEFELLER SR. PURSUED one purpose in his life—to organize the oil industry by horizontally and vertically integrating it under his company Standard Oil. His rigid daily schedule enabled him to work tirelessly to improve efficiency, cut costs, innovate, establish the first multinational company, and build the first modern corporation. He had the vision to take long-term risks and hire top talent to run parts of the business.

Here is one example of his relentless pursuit of purpose. In 1870, the Standard Oil Company owned one refinery in Cleveland, Ohio, a fleet of railroad tank cars, warehouses, and a barrel-making plant. Nevertheless, Rockefeller desired a more organized market, so he decided to acquire the twenty-six rival refineries located around Cleveland. His first step was to create an alliance with the three most powerful railroads that shipped the oil from Pennsylvania to the plants. The South Improvement Company, of which he was a founding member, enabled him to control oil prices, the shipment of oil to his refinery, and the transportation of oil to his rivals. The South Improvement Company enabled Rockefeller to grow his market share while limiting the profits of his competition. Eventually, in 1872, Rockefeller started buying out the other refineries as they struggled with their profitability. Within six months, he had acquired twenty-one out of the twenty-six refineries and organized the oil industry in America. By the end of the year, Standard Oil was the largest oil refiner in the world; Rockefeller was thirty-one years old.

Rockefeller didn't stop with Cleveland and the Pennsylvania oil fields, however. His pursuit of his purpose was wildly successful—at one time, Standard Oil controlled 90 percent of the world's oil production. The market was organized under Rockefeller and his company. However, in 1911, the US government broke Standard Oil into thirty-four new companies in an effort to split the monopoly and increase competition in the marketplace. While he faced setbacks, Rockefeller's single-minded purpose made him the wealthiest American ever, worth $14.9 billion in 1913 ($391 billion in today's dollars).

John D. Rockefeller is both a complex and contradictory person; however, his pursuit of purpose enabled him to be one of the greatest businesspeople of all time. Rockefeller had grit, or "the will to persevere to achieve long-term goals."

One underlying aspect of grit is understanding and living your personal purpose. At its simplest, your personal purpose is your *why*. It defines who you are and reflects your passions and values. Understanding your personal purpose, or *why*, helps you improve your goal setting, build resilience, and deal with the fear of failure. Movies and books can inspire your personal purpose. Introspection can also help you understand your personal purpose better.

PERSONAL PURPOSE INSPIRATION—MOVIES

Sometimes it is hard to determine your personal purpose, and movies are a great way to examine other people's personal purpose to help find your own. Below are six gritty movies that inspire me and I hope will inspire you to develop your personal purpose.

- *Prefontaine.* Steve Prefontaine (played by Jared Leto) was a track athlete who was determined to be the greatest long-distance runner in American history. He was an NCAA champion six times and came in fourth in 5,000-meter race at the 1972 Olympic Games.
- *42.* Jackie Robinson (played by the late Chadwick Boseman) was determined to prove that Black athletes could play and excel in Major League Baseball. Later, Robinson used his voice to help the civil rights movement.
- *Zero Dark Thirty.* Maya (played by Jessica Chastain), a CIA analyst, perseveres and develops the intelligence that enabled special operations forces to launch the raid on the Abbottabad compound that killed Osama Bin Laden.
- *John Wick.* After his wife dies of an illness and his dog is killed by members of the Russian mafia, an assassin, John Wick (played by Keanu Reeves), comes out of retirement and is unwavering in his efforts to destroy the entire Russian mob.
- *The Martian.* Mark Watney (played by Matt Damon) is an astronaut who is stranded on Mars. He is focused on surviving, getting rescued, and returning to Earth.
- *Wonder.* August "Auggie" Pullman (played by Jacob Tremblay) is a ten-year-old boy with a genetic deformity who attends a private school for the first time. He is determined to fit in.

There are hundreds of other movies that inspire people to understand and live their purpose. Find the one that inspires you, watch it (or rewatch it), and see how you can apply the main character's purpose to your life.

PERSONAL PURPOSE INSPIRATION—BOOKS

Great leaders are readers. Leaders like Mark Cuban, Warren Buffett, Oprah Winfrey, and Bill Gates make reading part of their daily habits. Reading (or listening to an audiobook) is a great way to grasp important concepts, understand new ideas, and access experiences that aren't your own. I have been a serious reader since I was a kid checking out books from the Delaware County Public Library, and I continue to read fiction, business, leadership, history, and science fiction books and magazines every day.

Here is a list of five gritty books that inspire me and hopefully help to inspire you to develop your personal purpose.

- *The Wright Brothers* by David McCullough is the well-written story of Orville and Wilbur Wright's focused pursuit of powered flight.
- *Hidden Figures* by Margot Lee Shetterly tells the stories of how Dorothy Vaughn, Mary Jackson, Katherine Johnson, and Christine Darden overcame racial and sexual prejudice to contribute to NASA's many successes in the Apollo program and beyond.
- *Titan* by Ron Chernow tells the story of John Rockefeller's single-minded development of the Standard Oil Company and his later philanthropic pursuits.
- *Into Thin Air* by Jon Krakauer is Krakauer's compelling personal account of the 1996 Mount Everest disaster.
- *Ashley's War: The Untold Story of a Team of Women Soldiers on the Special Operations Battlefield* by Gayle Tzemach Lemmon tells the story of the life and combat death of

> Lieutenant Ashley White, who was determined to serve and excel as a woman working with special operations forces in Afghanistan.

Leaders are busy, and deciding where to spend your time is one of the biggest decisions you make. Spending your time reading a book that expands your horizons, inspires you, enhances your grit, and develops a deeper understanding of your purpose is always a worthwhile use of your time.

PERSONAL PURPOSE EXERCISE

Finding and pursuing your purpose, or your personal *why*, is fundamental in developing your grit. You may already have a grasp of your personal purpose. If you don't, or you want to confirm it, try this four-step, fifteen-minute exercise to find your personal purpose.

First, identify your five core values. Core values are your fundamental beliefs and principles. Select five from this list, or develop your own:

Achievement	Expertise	Pragmatism
Adventure	Honesty	Relationships
Commitment	Independence	Responsibility
Community	Inspiration	Security
Consistency	Integrity	Self-control
Courage	Kindness	Self-discipline
Creativity	Loyalty	Spirituality
Education	Motivation	Tradition
Efficiency	Optimism	Reliability
Enjoyment	Pessimism	Reputation
Enthusiasm	Positivity	Vitality

> *For example, one client decided her values were adventure, creativity, positivity, and relationships.*

Then, rank order the values with the first being your most deeply held value.

> *For instance, the client decided her priorities were relationships, adventure, creativity, and positivity.*

Now, write a sentence or two which customizes the value to your situation or environment.

> *For example, her first three values statements were:*
>
> 1. *Relationships: I invest regularly in developing close connections with my family and my friends.*
> 2. *Adventure: I value trying new things, exploring new places and experiences, and pushing myself out of the comfort zone.*
> 3. *Creativity: I value opportunities to express my ideas, reactions, and observations.*

Once you have selected, customized, and rank ordered your values, use them to build a purpose statement.

> *Finally, she decided her purpose statement was, "To live an adventuresome and creative life while building close connections with those who are important to me."*

Share your personal purpose with your close friends and family. Ask for their feedback. Then display your personal purpose where you can see it every day, like a note on the refrigerator or on your bathroom mirror.

How did it work out for the client who did the personal purpose statement exercise? She finally went on the African safari that she had been putting off for years with her family. She's currently planning her next adventure—a trip to New Zealand with college friends.

OBSTACLE

The easiest part of finding your personal purpose is developing it using this exercise. The more challenging part is living up to your lofty goals. Once you develop your purpose, you may want to make time every December to evaluate how you lived up to your purpose during the year. You may discover that you aren't as creative as you had hoped you'd be. Or your commitment to sustaining relationships fell a little short. Understanding the gap between your purpose and your actions is helpful in improving how you live your purpose. Due to the reflection, you may decide to modify your purpose based on your evolving environment. Big life events like marriage, having children, or taking a new job can spark a significant reevaluation of your purpose. Living your personal purpose is a daily challenge.

CONCLUSION

The foundation for the grittiest people I know is their understanding and living of their personal purpose. John D. Rockefeller lived his purpose of organizing the oil industry under the Standard Oil Company. You may not follow your personal purpose to the extreme that Rockefeller did, but watching movies, reading books, or doing the personal purpose exercise can help you gain insight into your personal purpose. Having your arms around your *why* helps improve your goal-setting, builds resilience, and develops your courage, which then allows you to go on the offensive and grow your grit.

Chapter 3

IMPROVE YOUR GOAL SETTING

The most difficult thing is the decision to act, the rest is merely tenacity. The fears are paper tigers. You can do anything you decide to do. You can act to change and control your life; and the procedure, the process is its own reward.

Amelia Earhart

AMELIA EARHART, ONE OF THE most famous women in the world in the 1920s and 1930s, made a career of flying, writing, and lecturing. Born in Atchison, Kansas, Earhart set numerous aviation records, including being the first woman to fly across the Atlantic Ocean (1928), the first woman (and second person, after Charles Lindbergh) to fly solo and nonstop across the Atlantic (1932), and the first person to fly from Honolulu to Oakland, California (1935). She received the Distinguished Flying Cross from the US government for her solo flight across the Atlantic. In addition to her exploits in the air, she was an advocate for women's equality, and helped form the Ninety-Nines, an organization for women pilots. Unfortunately, she went missing during an attempt to circumnavigate the globe at the equator in 1937. The first woman to circumnavigate the globe, Jerrie Mock, didn't accomplish the feat until 1964.

Earhart encompasses almost all the aspects of grit in the quote. She had a purpose. She had a goal. She had perseverance, or what she calls "tenacity." She had the courage to manage her fears by adopting a learning orientation to the process. In short, she had grit.

Between 1930 and 1935, Earhart set seven women's speed and distance aviation records in a variety of aircraft. In both 1932 and 1933, she set the solo, nonstop, and transcontinental speed records for women pilots. Each attempt required careful goal setting and planning to push the envelope and accomplish the record. As Earhart remarked, "Preparation, I have often said, is rightly two-thirds of any venture."

A goal is an idea of what things will look like in the future, or a desired result that a person or a group of people envision, plan, and commit to achieve. The second part of growing your grit is setting a goal. In contrast to Amelia Earhart, most people are bad at setting goals and reaching them. Every December when we turn the calendar to the new year, many people set goals by creating their New Year's resolution. Yet, according to research, only 8 percent of all people ever feel that they are successful in achieving their goals, and 42 percent give up on their resolution before February first. I see this every year at the gym—it's packed in January, but come February, I only see the regular patrons. People fail at achieving their goals because they lack the tools to properly set goals. Improving your goal-setting techniques can help you accomplish not just your New Year's resolution, but more for yourself, more for your family, and more at work.

I have found that there are four things that help improve goal setting—defining your goal, breaking your goal down into steps, thinking through the most likely obstacle to achieving your goal, and, lastly, communicating your goal. Using these tools will increase the likelihood of accomplishing your goal.

SMART GOALS

A great way to define a goal is to use the mnemonic device SMART. Defining a SMART goal means that the goal is Specific, Measurable, Attainable, Relevant, and Time bound. Some questions to ask yourself as you develop a SMART goal:

- Specific: What will be accomplished? What actions will you take?
- Measurable: What data will measure the goal? (How much? How well?)
- Achievable: Is the goal doable? Do you have the necessary skills and resources?
- Relevant: How does the goal align with broader goals? Does it align with your purpose? Why is the result important?
- Time bound: What is the time frame for accomplishing the goal?

Using the SMART tool sharpens your goals and gives you a greater chance of accomplishing them. Let's look at three examples of SMART goals.

Example #1

Let's say your goal is to "improve your fitness." That isn't a SMART goal, but it can be transformed into one. A better, SMART goal would be, "For the year, I want to walk every day, workout in the gym on Monday, Wednesday, and Friday, and not eat dessert during the months of January and February." The new goal is specific, measurable, and time bound. If it aligns with your personal purpose and is realistic, it qualifies as a SMART goal.

Example #2

Let's say your goal is to "be seen as a leader in the company." Once again, not a SMART goal, but it can also be reworked. A better, SMART goal would be, "Build my leadership skills by working on projects that increase my opportunities for vision and goal setting, enable me to create and manage change, and improve my strategic thought competencies by the end of the year; have my boss and one other person senior to me recognize my growth as a leader." The new goal is specific, measurable, and time bound. This goal, however, may need some steps or sub-tasks (see below) to work through to accomplish the goal.

Example #3

Let's say your goal is to "get promoted at work this year." Not SMART, but it can be. A better, SMART goal would be "Identify my gaps in growing as a data scientist and grow my skills to a level that by the end of the year, people across my division recognize me as the subject matter expert on this topic." This goal adds greater specificity, is measurable, and is time bound. Specific sub-tasks or steps (see below) will be needed to accomplish this goal.

Once you have created a SMART goal, it is worth evaluating if it is a stretch goal, which is a goal that sets a target beyond your own or other's expectations. Being the first woman and second person to fly solo across the Atlantic was a stretch goal for Amelia Earhart. Grit is typically developed in the pursuit of a stretch goal as you push your boundaries.

Steps

Once you have a SMART goal, break it down into steps. During the Apollo 13 mission, after the oxygen tank exploded in space, Gene Kranz famously told the team at Mission Control, "Let's work the problem, people. Let's not make things worse by guessing." Kranz's statement captures NASA's culture perfectly. Break a SMART goal down into steps and start working them as you would when confronted with any big problem. During the Apollo 13 crisis, NASA engineers broke down the seemingly single problem of bringing the astronauts home safely in to manageable steps: dealing with limited power and a shortage of water, removing carbon dioxide from the spacecraft, powering up the command module, and guiding the spacecraft back to Earth. Like NASA, break the problem down and work each smaller problem.

Another way to break a goal down into steps is to think about how you would work the problem backward. In other words, work from the accomplishment of the goal back to where you are today. Take the goal and think through the last step you will need to do before you achieve it, then the previous, and then the previous. Once you get to your start point and have thought through the entire process, you are ready to put the plan into action.

CHALLENGES

Challenges are going to occur with trying to achieve any goal. It is important to identify and think through the most likely obstacle you will encounter. List every obstacle you think you might encounter. The challenges I always encounter are too many distractions, lack of commitment, not measuring your progress, family commitments, no outlined milestones, underestimating the time commitment, or procrastination. You may encounter others; write them down.

Once you have your list of challenges, go through the list and prioritize it from the most likely to the least likely. When you're comfortable with the most likely challenge, develop two ways to overcome it. You may want to add these techniques to your list of steps or milestones on the way to accomplish your goal.

COMMUNICATE YOUR GOAL

The simple act of writing the goal down can help energize your gritty journey to achieve it. Write your goal on a sticky note and put it in your cubicle or in your house where you will see it. Seeing it every day supports accountability and helps you build momentum and perseverance.

If writing it down doesn't spark accountability, another approach you can try is telling your goal to a friend or family member—but make sure you choose the person wisely because it matters. A recent study found that people have a greater goal commitment and accountability when they tell their goal to someone they believe has a higher status than themselves. Howard Klein, an Ohio State University business professor, says, "Contrary to what you may have heard, in most cases you get more benefit from sharing your goal than if you don't—as long as you share it with someone whose opinion you value." Telling a person you respect works because you care about their opinion and don't want them to think less of you should you not attain your goal.

OBSTACLE—TIME

The biggest obstacle to achieving any goal is finding the time to do the steps needed to achieve it. Once you've committed to your plan of action, pull out your calendar and block time to accomplish each of the steps. Making time to accomplish the new goal may require figuring out what needs to be cancelled. Make sure you schedule time to evaluate your progress toward the goal and assess if the goal is still the proper objective.

One of your biggest decisions as a leader is where and how you spend your time. Your personal operating rhythm is the cadence of meetings, engagements with clients, engagements with your boss, and engagements with the team that helps drive you to meet your objectives. As part of this goal setting, it may be worthwhile to review your personal calendar for the past month.

Divide the different events on your calendar into three categories: the productive uses of your time (i.e., the ones that are helping you achieve the goal), the time wasters (those that don't help you achieve the goal), and what tasks could have been done by others (delegate). Eliminate the time wasters from your calendar for the next month, delegate those tasks that can be done by others, and focus on maximizing the productive use of your time.

Making time on your calendar to accomplish your goals, as well as optimizing your personal battle rhythm are critical steps in accomplishing any goal.

CONCLUSION

Establishing a goal is the second part in growing your grit or "the will to persevere to achieve long-term goals." Enhance your goal setting by defining your goals using the mnemonic device SMART (Specific, Measurable, Achievable, Relevant, Time bound); break your goal down into steps; think through the most likely obstacle that will prevent you from achieving it; communicate it; and, finally, put time on the calendar to work toward it. Once you have a goal, this approach makes it easier to develop and improve your perseverance, your resilience, your courage to deal with the fear of failure, and your motivation.

Whether you use your goal to push boundaries like Amelia Earhart or use it to make and keep a New Year's resolution or any other goal you set out to achieve is up to you. But first, you have to establish the goal and set yourself up to be successful.

Chapter 4

ENHANCE YOUR PERSEVERANCE

"I ended up persevering through roadblocks by just not giving up. I used a lot of persistence balanced with humor balanced with vulnerability and I asked people to help."

Sara Blakely, founder and CEO of Spanx

SARA BLAKELY IS THE FOUNDER and owner of Spanx, a private company that makes slimming undergarments for men and women. In 2012, she joined the ranks of the *Forbes* magazine's World's Billionaires List as the youngest, self-made woman billionaire. Growing her company from a side hustle out of her apartment to a global giant, Sara exhibited incredible persistence.

While working at the office supply company Danka (now part of Ricoh) as a salesperson and national sales trainer, Blakely identified a problem she knew needed to be solved. She liked the slimming effect of panty hose but not the heat during the summer, so she cut the feet off a pair of panty hose and wore them underneath a pair of slacks, and voila! Spanx was born. She spent the next two years refining the idea until she was ready to start the company as a side project. To grow the company, she filed her own patent for the design, cold-called factories to manufacture the product, designed the packaging, created her own website, called fashion reporters to get the company positive exposure, and fulfilled orders from her living room.

Critical to Blakely's success was the persistence she had acquired selling office products door-to-door for Danka. She drew on those memories of successes and failures to develop the fortitude to call on retailers to carry Spanx. She got rejected a lot, but she made a few sales and remained persistent. She went to malls on the weekend, set up a booth, and sold Spanx directly to customers. Slowly, her customer base grew through her persistence.

She also shipped several free samples to Oprah Winfrey's stylist Andre Walker. Walker shared them with Oprah, who liked them so much that she named them one of her favorite products in 2000. Spanx sales exploded overnight, earning the company $4 million in its first year. It has been profitable every year and has never taken investment capital.

Blakely quit Danka after Oprah. To help grow the company, she also hired talent to bridge her gaps. Employee #5 at Spanx was Laurie Ann Goldman, a ten-year veteran of Coca-Cola. Goldman provided Spanx the big-company perspective that helped Blakely scale and run the company. Sara kept building momentum in Spanx—last year the company had $400 million in revenue.

Over the past twenty years, Sara Blakely exhibited perseverance by building on small, gritty wins and creating momentum for herself and Spanx.

PERSEVERANCE

Perseverance is persistence in doing something difficult. In December of 2020, I joined the Rapha Festive 500, which has a simple premise—ride 500 kilometers (310 miles) between Christmas Eve and New Year's Eve (eight days) to be eligible to win a bicycle. To keep things interesting, Rapha (a cycling sportswear company) would post on Strava (an app that tracks exercise via GPS data and has multiple social networking features) when I had completed 20, 40, 60, and 80 percent of the Rapha Festive 500.

Until that point, I had never ridden more than 275 miles in eight days. While I know there are some incredible cyclists out there who have ridden a lot farther than I have, I am proud to say that I rode 347 miles during the Rapha Festival 500. With my longest day at 64.5 miles and my shortest at 25 miles, I rode every day, averaging 43 miles per day. It required all of my perseverance, and more, to accomplish that achievement.

So how did I develop the perseverance to ride 347 miles in eight days? How can you develop more perseverance to apply toward your next tough, long-term task? I have found three things exceptionally helpful in building perseverance—small wins, remembering past persistence, and building momentum.

First, I started with small wins. In addition to grit being an acquired skill, it is transferable. If you are gritty in one area, it can transfer to another. For me, walking my dog, Samantha, daily is a small, gritty win. Every day that I get out of bed and walk the dog, I claim it as a small victory. Plus, the neighbors see me, so there is a social accountability aspect to doing the walks as well. As I struggled to get myself motivated to ride the bike, I drew upon the perseverance and grit I had gained walking Samantha.

Second, remember past persistence. Drawing on memories of past persistent efforts is a great way to increase your perseverance. Think about one of your gritty accomplishments that you are particularly proud of. It could be something like running a marathon, writing a book, graduating from college, or learning how to play the guitar. Whatever it was, visualize the actions, behaviors, and habits that it took to accomplish that goal. Once you have thought through the past persistence and the success that came from your hard work, the current challenge shouldn't seem so daunting.

As I pedaled my bike in December, I drew upon my past persistence efforts, and one memory, in particular, was helpful. In 2014, I got into deadlifting. I read everything I could on it; I got coaches to look at my technique and watched countless YouTube videos to perfect my form. More importantly, I was persistent and made sure that every week I did five sets of five deadlifts, adding a little weight to my lifts each week. Eventually, I was able to deadlift my goal of 405 pounds.

Finally, build momentum. Momentum is a powerful tool that makes it difficult to stop things once they are set in motion. In his book *Good to Great*, Jim Collins calls momentum in a corporate environment the "flywheel effect." He defines the flywheel as the process that turns good companies into great companies as "a cumulative process—step by step, action by action, decision by decision, turn by turn of the flywheel—that adds up to sustained and spectacular results."

A subset of momentum, much like the flywheel, is the streak. A streak in this context means to do something on consecutive days without fail. For instance, Ron Hill, a three-time Olympic runner for Great Britain, ran at least one mile a day for fifty-two years and thirty-nine days. It is the longest running streak ever. Streaks are so powerful that there is a web page and organization dedicated to tracking runners' streaks. It is called Streak Running International. Check it out.

Want to write a book? Write every day for ninety days. Put up a calendar and cross the days off one by one so you can see a visual representation of the streak. Want to do "Dry January?" Treat it as a streak of not drinking alcohol for thirty-one days. Tell a friend you are doing it, and text or email every day you don't drink for more accountability. Want to get healthier? Work out every day for a month. To get your streak going, you may want to work out at the same time each day for the first week. Want to save money? Automatically transfer money from each paycheck to a savings account or 401k plan.

For me personally, when I set out on the gritty journey of completing the Rapha Festival 500, I knew the goal, but the path to achieving the goal wasn't clear. However, I knew riding the bike every day would get me closer to the goal. Once I got through the first three days, the momentum I had generated and the power of the streak of riding every day made it difficult to stop, even when I was tired and sore. The streak of needing to put in miles every day created momentum and helped get me across the finish line. Together, the momentum and power of the streak helped me to go farther in eight days than I had ever done before.

OBSTACLE

One of the biggest obstacles to perseverance is the chaos of our modern life. There are a million priorities—work, family, hobbies, friends, health, and entertainment—all competing for attention. At different periods in my life, I've felt like the plate spinner at the circus with only enough time to rush from plate to plate to keep each spinning and the whole thing from crashing to the ground. But simplifying one thing, like starting and maintaining a streak—writing one page a day or working ten minutes a day on a big project or running one mile a day—can help dissipate some of the chaos, enhance your persistence, and help you achieve a long-term goal.

CONCLUSION

Improving your perseverance isn't easy. Whether you are building an undergarments company out of your apartment, riding your bike 347 miles in eight days, or attempting to go thirty-one days without alcohol, you can use small wins, remember past persistence, and capitalize on momentum to forge your perseverance. Discover what technique works for you to enhance your perseverance, go on the offense, and grow your grit.

Chapter 5

DEVELOP YOUR RESILIENCE

"I vowed I wouldn't ever let anyone destroy me again. I was going to work at it every day, so hard that I would be the toughest guy in the world. By the end of practice, I wanted to be physically tired, to know that I'd been through a workout. If I wasn't tired, I must have cheated somehow, so I stayed a little longer."

Dan Gable, Olympic gold medal wrestler

DAN GABLE IS A FORMER American freestyle wrestler and coach. From 1967 to 1970, Gable attended Iowa State University, where he won two NCAA championships. He compiled a collegiate record of 117–1, with his only loss coming at the NCAA championship in his last match as a collegiate wrestler. At Northwestern University on March 28, 1970, an unknown sophomore, Larry Owings, stepped onto the mat against Gable, the best wrestler in the nation. Owings had dropped two weight classes so he could wrestle the best. At stake was the NCAA championship. Nine minutes later, Owings won the match 13–11.

Losing to Owings could have derailed Gable. It was the first time he had lost in eight years on the wrestling mat. Instead, he bounced back and used the loss to focus his intensity on being the best he could possibly be at international wrestling. As an elite athlete, he was dialed in on his sleep, nutrition, and physical fitness. But he focused on building his mindset and his mindfulness. To develop both, he would not only visualize upcoming matches with his opponent, but also his opponent's workouts so he could be sure he was working out more than the competition. Gable grew his already legendary grit and resilience to a higher level.

Gable even admits that "it would take me years to realize this, but I wouldn't have become a great wrestler and a great coach—a legend in the sport—without that match." He won the gold medal in the 68 kg (150 lb) weight class at the 1972 Olympic games in Munich without giving up a point in six straight matches against the world's best wrestlers. Dan Gable's story is an example of someone with strong resilience and an enormous amount of grit.

As you set off to accomplish a gritty goal you will inevitably experience setbacks. Are you prepared to deal with them, or are they going to derail you? How are you going to overcome them? Are you going to be like Dan Gable who gets even better after a defeat? Resilience is the capacity to recover from difficulties or setbacks. It is the boxer who gets knocked down but gets back on his feet to fight another round. More importantly, it is a mindset. A resilience mindset comes from living your personal purpose, as well as making sure you are getting the proper sleep, nutrition, physical fitness, social interaction, and you are practicing mindfulness.

PERSONAL PURPOSE, GOALS, AND RESILIENCE

It is helpful to pause and think about your personal purpose or your *why*. Your *why* should inspire you. Your *why* should inspire others. By clearly outlining, understanding, and living your personal purpose, you are better equipped to be resilient when facing obstacles. If you haven't gone through the steps of identifying your *why* or your current *why* doesn't inspire you, I encourage you to return to Chapter 2 and go through the personal purpose exercise.

Once your personal purpose is in focus, the next step is to make sure your goals are helping you move closer to achieving your purpose. As discussed earlier, it is critical to block time in your busy schedule to make progress toward achieving them. And having a goal connected to your personal purpose increases your personal alignment and improves your resiliency when you face the inevitable setback. If your goal is lacking in some aspect, or isn't tied to your purpose, go back to Chapter 3 and use the ideas to improve your goal setting.

Resiliency is more than a mental mindset, however. There are five key physiological aspects to improving resiliency and growing grit: sleep, nutrition, physical fitness, social interaction, and mindfulness. Dial them all in, like Dan Gable, and you will be well on your way to being to bounce back from any setback.

Sleep

The American football coach Vince Lombardi allegedly said, "Fatigue makes cowards of us all." And he is right. Everyone has made bad decisions or abandoned tough challenges when they were tired.

The US Army has a culture of performing on limited sleep. I know from my experience in the army that the need to do physical fitness early in the morning and the responsibilities of being a leader meant that I lived on six hours of sleep a night and lots of coffee. I now realize that my insufficient sleep inhibited my performance, hindered my recovery from my physical fitness, and made me irritable.

The average person needs at least seven hours of sleep a night. But a recent study revealed that 35 percent of men and 34 percent of women report getting less than seven hours of sleep at least one night a week. I just checked my sleep app, and this week I had one night where I got six hours and nine minutes of sleep. Afterward I looked at my daily schedule for that day and could see the impact—I only wrote 500 words in a blog post and made one business call all day; not my most productive day.

Sleep affects every aspect of your overall health and performance. Quality sleep helps improve your memory, promotes tissue repair, strengthens your immune system, and grows grit. There are two processes involved in sleep regulation: sleep drive and the circadian rhythm. Sleep drive is the need for your body to go to sleep to remove the sleep-promoting metabolites that build up in the brain while you are awake. The circadian rhythm is the internal clock for sleep and wake cycles and is based on daylight and darkness.

It's not always possible to get seven hours of sleep, but optimizing the quality of your sleep can make whatever you are getting the best possible. No matter how much sleep you are getting, there are several proven ways to improve the quality of your sleep:

- Eliminate all light sources in the bedroom.
- Eliminate screen time thirty minutes before bedtime.
- No food after 7:00 p.m.
- No caffeine after 3:30 p.m.
- Set the temperature in the bedroom to sixty-eight degrees.
- Try to go to bed at the same time every night.

If you can't fall asleep, I have found that taking five mg of melatonin is helpful and doesn't leave me with any side effects.

Prescription sleep aides tend to make me feel groggy the following morning.

Sleep is critical for your health and performance. If you can't get the seven or more hours of sleep your body needs, try to improve the quality of your sleep. Improving your sleep builds your resilience, improves your energy, enhances your decision-making and thinking, and helps grow your grit. Commit to making a change and improving the quality and quantity of your sleep.

Nutrition

Almost 31 percent of Americans are overweight. There are a million diets out there. Keto, Paleo, Atkins, Grapefruit, and eating gluten-free all have their devotees. However, it is difficult to maintain restrictive eating patterns for long periods of time. Eating healthy helps you maintain your energy, optimize your daily mental and physical performance, and build your resilience.

At its essence, healthy eating is making good food choices on a daily and weekly basis. Healthy eating is a habit. For me, eating healthy starts at the grocery store—if I don't have it in the pantry or refrigerator, I won't eat it.

The average person consumes about twenty different foods per week. Not a believer? Track your food for a week and you will see the patterns emerge. Real foods, like vegetables, meat, fruit, and grains are so much better for you than processed foods. If, after a week of tracking your food, your diet already consists of tuna, salmon, apples, vegetables, eggs, chicken, almonds, oatmeal, and blueberries, you are well on your way to eating healthy.

Here are seven proven tips to eat healthier:

- Track your food intake for a week in a journal or on an app.
- Drink 2.5 liters (2.6 quarts) of water per day.

- Don't shop hungry. Eat something before you go to the grocery.
- Use a shopping list.
- Shop the perimeter of the grocery (where the real food—vegetables, fruit, meat) is before you hit the aisles (where the processed food is).
- Prepare your food for the week on Sunday. Many people prepare their breakfast and lunch for the week so they are more efficient and make good food choices.
- Snack on fruits or almonds.

At the end of the day, focus on eating real foods and making good food choices that make you feel and perform your best. Eating Better foods enhances performance, helps your recovery from tough workouts, builds your resilience, and grows your grit. Whether you use these ideas or others, eating healthier will pay dividends on your waistline and for your resilience.

Physical Fitness

Proper exercise increases performance, improves stamina, enhances your metabolism, improves sleep, increases physical resiliency, and decreases injuries. People gain huge health benefits when they exercise. In fact, according to recent research, executives who are physically fit are considered to be more effective leaders than those who are out of shape.

I have been an athlete all my life. One of my favorite things about the army was that we got paid to work out for ninety minutes a day. Heck, I was almost a professional athlete! Over the past thirty years my athletic pursuits went beyond the army too. I've competed in running races, bicycle races, swimming competitions, and triathlons.

The single biggest obstacle to better physical fitness is time. Everyone is busy with life, work, family, and friends. For the last five years I have used a philosophy that no matter how busy I am, I can always find ten minutes to do some sort of physical activity each day. This could be walking up and down a set of stairs five times, or doing three sets of push-ups, sit-ups, and air squats in my hotel room. If I complete ten minutes of exercise, I am content. But committing to the ten minutes a day helps me overcome the mental hurdle of the huge time commitment of driving to the gym, working out, and driving home (or doing the two-hour bike ride). While I often get more than ten minutes, the ten-minutes-a-day commitment has made physical fitness a consistent, daily habit no matter how busy I am or what setbacks I face. (More on habits in Chapter 8)

In the grand scheme of things, it really doesn't matter what methods you use to pursue better physical fitness. Running, biking, swimming, rowing, cross-country skiing, tennis, and hiking all improve your aerobic and anaerobic fitness. Weightlifting, plyometrics, yoga, and body weight exercises improve your strength and flexibility. CrossFit, obstacle courses, P90X, and Orange Theory Fitness improve your aerobic and anerobic fitness as well as your strength. The most important thing is that you do something.

There are hundreds of great books and websites on physical fitness. If you don't have a favorite author, construct your own routine using this basic concept. A great workout should be comprised of either aerobic or anaerobic activity as well as exercises from one to all six of the movements:

- Aerobic activity: jogging, walking, bicycle riding, and swimming.
- Anerobic activity: short, intense activity like sprints, sled drag or sled push, rowing sprints, Jacob's ladder, and the assault bike.
- Squat movement: air squats, front squats, rear squats, lunge, and box jump.

- Deadlift movement: think deadlift or kettlebell swing.
- Press movement: think bench press, push-up, or overhead press.
- Pull movement: pull-up, chin-up, or lateral pull down.
- Weighted carry: farmer's carry (heavy object in both hands), suitcase carry (heavy object in one hand), or overheard carry (heavy object in one hand overhead).
- Abdominal movement: plank, crunch, leg lift, or Turkish getup.

A simple workout that I like to do when I am travelling is three to five rounds of:

- 10 push-ups
- 10 sit-ups or crunches
- 10 air squats
- 30 seconds of plank
- Running in place for three minutes or running up and down a flight of stairs for three minutes

Do physical fitness that excites you and keeps you interested. When you get bored, mix it up or try something new. But do some physical fitness every day. Improving your fitness will build your stamina, your decision-making, your resilience, and your grit. Committing to doing ten minutes a day is a great place to start. Whether you use these fitness concepts or others, it is more important to do something rather than nothing.

Social Interaction

Building and maintaining relationships with friends and family has incredible benefits for your mental health, resilience, and grit. Conventional wisdom says that you are shaped by the five people you spend the most time with. These relationships enable you to share ideas, grow mentally, de-stress, and decrease depression. Although face-to-face relationships are the most powerful, today's technology—Zoom, Microsoft Teams, emails, texts, and phone calls—can still help nurture relationships and increase social interaction.

Once again, the obstacle to having social interaction and building relationships is time. Budget time each week to interact and build your relationships. Make it part of your habits. Social interaction helps to build your performance, resilience, and grit.

Improving your social interactions can help you to bounce back and accomplish your gritty goals. These connections will enable you to thrive in the chaos of life, build your resilience, and accomplish your gritty goals. Whether you use these techniques or others, the time spent building connections with co-workers, friends, and family is always well spent.

Mindfulness

Mindfulness, or meditation, play an important role in building resilience. Mindfulness means paying attention on purpose, in the present moment, without judgment. Throughout the ages, samurai, medieval knights, and monks have practiced forms of mindfulness to increase their focus, decision-making, and resilience. The actor and martial arts expert Bruce Lee was a big proponent of mindfulness. As Dan Harris, author of *10% Happier,* writes, "It can give you a 10 percent mental advantage." In today's distracted environment, with computers, TVs, email, texts, Microsoft Teams, Slack, and WhatsApp all demanding our attention, it is even more important to practice mindfulness.

Although simple in concept, practicing mindfulness is challenging. Mindfulness is emptying your mind from everything distracting and being fully present for a short amount of time.

There are dozens of tools and techniques to do this, but, personally, I like this one best:

1. Sit in a chair or lie down. Get comfortable. Set your watch or phone alarm for five minutes.
2. Close your eyes.
3. Focus on the sensation of your breath as it goes in and out.
4. Here is the big secret: your mind is going to wander. When it does, just forgive yourself, mentally note these external thoughts, and return to focusing on your breathing. The work and the benefit happen when you catch your mind wandering and bring it back. Like doing repetitions at the gym, the more you practice, the better you will get and the longer you can go without your mind wandering.

Improving your ability to remain present and focused will enable you to thrive in the chaos of life, build your resilience, and accomplish your gritty goals. Whether you use this technique or another, it is worth sharpening your mind for five minutes per day.

OBSTACLE

Hundreds of sources prompt us to develop a resilient mindset, sleep better, eat healthier, work out, develop social connections, and practice mindfulness, but the people that put these all together are few and far between. It isn't easy. Many people take an all-or-nothing approach to these ideas. Instead, I ask you to consider the small, incremental approach. Find one little thing you can do better, make it easy to do, and then consistently do it over and over until it is a habit. Then use the momentum from one small win to build another small win. And then build another and then another. Over time you can make some significant changes by working small problems.

CONCLUSION

You are inevitably going to face setbacks when you strive to accomplish a gritty goal. Building your resilience, both mentally and physically, is one way to make sure you are ready to handle whatever is thrown at you. Bounce back and keep putting one foot in front of the other, stronger than you were before.

Dan Gable rebounded from being beat by Larry Owings to take his wrestling skills to the next level. Although you aren't training for the Olympics, go on the offensive and enhance your resilience by understanding and living your personal purpose as well as ensuring you are getting the proper sleep, nutrition, physical fitness, social interaction, and mindfulness. Grow your grit.

Chapter 6

FORGE STRONGER COURAGE

"Thinking of my achievements to date gives me courage in all situations—particularly being promoted to principal ballerina of the American Ballet Theatre. It was not only an achievement for me but for the scores of black women who were incredibly talented and deserving but never had the opportunity. I thank Under Armour for recognizing this and having me as an Under Armour athlete to inspire women everywhere!"

Misty Copeland, ballerina

ONE OF SIX CHILDREN RAISED by a single mother, Misty Copeland became the first African American to be named principal ballerina for the American Ballet Theater (ABT), one of the three best classical ballet companies in the United States. It was not an easy road for Copeland. She had to overcome a vertebrae fracture, a tibia fracture, and over a decade of work until she was selected as a principal dancer. Fear of failure shadowed her throughout her odyssey.

Today, Copeland is the most famous ballerina in the United States. To get to this position, she leveraged her perseverance, saying, "I may not be there yet, but I am closer than I was yesterday." She is known for her many hours spent in the studio, as well as using Pilates, barre a terre, and swimming to build her strength and agility. She also had to overcome ballet's bias against Black dancers.

Even as a principal dancer, Copeland used her courage to deal with her fear of failure. As the Swan Queen in the ABT production of *Swan Lake*, a YouTube video of her went viral when she failed to execute the thirty-two fouettés properly. Rather than deny it, she embraced the failure. She posted the video to her Instagram account and added a comment that "I will forever be a work in progress and will never stop learning." Focusing on the learning process, like Copeland does, is a powerful tool to build your courage.

Copeland's grit has helped her succeed off the stage as well. She was in the Disney movie *Nutcracker and the Four Realms* and danced in a Diet Dr. Pepper ad. She is a sponsored athlete for the brand Under Armour. In 2017 she became one of the first non-model spokespeople for an Estee Lauder fragrance campaign. Finally, she has written three books—*Life in Motion: An Unlikely Ballerina*, *Ballerina Body: Dancing and Eating Your Way to a Leaner, Stronger, and More Graceful You*, and a children's book, *Firebird*.

Copeland's road to the top wasn't easy. Using her grit and courage, Misty Copeland dealt with her fear of failure and worked her way to the pinnacle of the ballet world.

COURAGE

Courage is the willingness to confront danger or uncertainty. In the case of grit, courage is demonstrated by managing the fear of failure. Gritty goals, like becoming the first African American principal ballerina, are typically stretch goals or targets that exceed what is expected. Each person has their own definition of a stretch goal. For some, it might be to make one sale a month. For the best salesperson in the company, it might be to make ten sales per month. Improving your courage is the fourth step in growing your personal grit.

Because the gritty goal usually exceeds expectations, fear of failure is a very real emotion that must be acknowledged and dealt with. For some, the fear of failure may manifest itself in numerous ways: a reluctance to try new things; self-sabotage such as procrastination, failure to follow-through, or anxiety; low self-confidence; or perfectionism, such as a willingness to try only those things that can be finished perfectly. As I have tried to accomplish tough, gritty goals, I have experienced all of those feelings. Overcoming that fear is a real challenge.

When I started my company, The Fivecoat Consulting Group (TFCG), in March 2020, I had a very real fear of failure. I know many entrepreneurs and small business owners experience this same fear. It was the first time I had started a company, the first time I didn't have a regular paycheck, and the pandemic had just started. Companies were eliminating outside consultants to preserve cash, and the business environment was extraordinarily tough. I had lots of anxiety, sleepless nights, and little confidence. My thoughts always turned to the idea of how useful people would find the company and the blog. Would people want to listen to me talk about leadership and grit? Would I be able to make ends meet? As I went through June, July, and August without a paying client, my anxiety only intensified.

Three techniques—listing my fears, reframing my definition of success and failure, and focusing on learning—helped me have the courage to deal with the fear of failure, especially when I didn't have any clients.

As Yoda, from the movie *Star Wars*, once said, "Named must your fear be before banish it you can." So, I listed my fears and developed a way to reduce some of the risk of each fear. To help build the list, I used some questions developed by Tim Ferris, noted author, podcaster, and entrepreneur. My responses follow each question in italics.

- Define your nightmare by thinking about what is the absolute worst that could happen?
  For me, it was the company not bringing in any clients and being forced to have to close TFCG because I was gradually exhausting my savings.

- Is any of this permanent?
  No, only a loss of some savings.

- What steps could I take to repair the damage?
  Find a corporate or contractor job to recover the savings I'd spent.

- What is a more probable outcome?
  The business helps people become better, grittier leaders while bringing in enough revenue for me to make ends meet.

- What are the outcomes or benefits, both temporary and permanent, of more probable scenarios?
  I learn new things as I create a company, I learn more about myself, and clients become grittier and better leaders.

- How much time will you spend on the new endeavor?
  I would commit everything to TFCG for one year. (This time frame also helped me with reframing my definition of success and failure.)

Second, I reframed my definitions of success and failure. The definition of success stayed the same, of course—have a thriving business where I was able to help people and businesses become grittier and better leaders. However, it took some work to reframe my definition of failure. I had failed at plenty of things in the military, like the first time I attempted Air Assault School (failed sling load inspection), the first time at Jumpmaster School (failed Jumpmaster Pre-Inspection), the first time through the Florida phase of Ranger School (failed patrols), and I wasn't selected during tryouts to serve in the 75th Ranger Regiment. Each of those experiences helped me learn and grow. So I took the same approach with TFCG—not acquiring enough clients to keep the business functioning became a learning experience instead of a failure.

I also had to separate the business failing from my self-esteem. The potential failure of TFCG would be a result, not a way to describe myself. Just because I "failed" at starting a business in the pandemic wouldn't mean I'm a failure as a person.

Finally, I focused on learning. Building and growing TFCG has become a learning experience. I've learned how to build my own website on Squarespace, twice; I've learned how to blog; I've learned how to use MailChimp to send out emails twice a week; I've learned how to create LinkedIn posts that would get 30,000+ views; I have learned how to make sales; and I have learned how to deliver quality webinars. Looking back over the first year of establishing a company, it was a phenomenal learning experience that helped me learn about building a small business, growing as a person, and growing my own grit.

CONCLUSION

Misty Copeland failed many times as she became the most recognized ballerina in the United States. Overcoming a tibia fracture at age thirty and returning to the highest level on stage is astonishing. I'm not in the same league as Misty, but I too have failed hundreds of times trying to reach professional and personal goals. Both of us developed courage to deal with that very real fear of failure. Whether you list your fears, reframe your definition of success and failure, or focus on the learning, you can and will enhance your courage. Having the courage to risk the fear of failure is another powerful step in growing your grit.

Chapter 7

UPGRADE YOUR MOTIVATION

"I've missed more than 9,000 shots in my career. I've lost almost 300 games. Twenty-six times, I've been trusted to take the game winning shot and missed. I've failed over and over and over again in my life. And that is why I succeed."

Michael Jordan, NBA Hall of Famer

MICHAEL JORDAN IS THE GREATEST National Basketball Association (NBA) player of all time, with six NBA championships, six NBA Finals Most Valuable Player (MVP) awards, and five NBA MVP awards; he also led the NBA in scoring ten times and won two Olympic gold medals. Jordan was physically gifted—six feet, six inches tall with a forty-four-inch vertical leap, plus strength, speed, and huge hands. But what took him to a different level were his extreme competitiveness, work ethic, and incredible perseverance. Jordan used his competitiveness in everything—in basketball, baseball, golf, and cards—to provide motivation, spark creativity, raise his performance, and accomplish his goals.

In addition to Jordan's competitiveness, he fueled his drive with a passion for the process of creating a winning team. Coach Phil Jackson was able to convince Jordan that he wasn't going to win a title on his talent alone; instead, he had to trust the process. Jackson's process used four tenets: the team had to prepare relentlessly through demanding practices and watching hours of game film, use the triangle offense to provide scoring opportunities, use tough defense to shut down opponents, and everyone would need to stay calm. Jordan quickly embraced the process, and six NBA championships followed.

Another technique he employed to fuel his motivation was to use an adversary. For example, Jordan still detests Isiah Thomas, another former NBA star, and uses this hatred to fuel his drive. Thomas was part of the Detroit Pistons team that beat the Chicago Bulls three years in a row in the playoffs, led an effort in an All-Star game to keep the ball away from Jordan, and didn't shake the Bulls' hands after a game. As Jordan famously says in *The Last Dance*, "I took that personally." Jordan used his hate to work extra hard to beat Isiah Thomas and the Pistons the following year. Leveraging your motivation, like in the case of Michael Jordan finding an adversary, can help fuel your grit.

SOME OF THE PSYCHOLOGY BEHIND MOTIVATION

Drive. Motivation. Catalyst. Power. Passion (this is what Angela Duckworth uses). Whatever you call it, growing your grit needs fuel. Intrinsic motivation and extrinsic motivation power the development of your grit. Finding your motivation is the sixth, and last step, in growing your grit. As you set out to accomplish a gritty goal, it is important to understand and acknowledge what is fueling your grit, what motivational tool works for you, which ones don't, and where you can turn for help when you hit an obstacle.

Intrinsic motivation is when a person pursues a goal or activity for its own sake without any external reward. Intrinsic motivation satisfies basic needs such as food, water, and shelter or higher needs such as autonomy, mastery, and purpose. Noted author Daniel Pink, in his book *Drive: The Surprising Truth About What Motivates Us,* argues that intrinsic motivation is usually the stronger source for drive. For instance, you may pursue a goal or activity because it makes you happy, you enjoy it, or it makes you feel satisfied. Intrinsic motivation works because it leverages your innate personal accountability and desire to learn. People have a deep desire to be in control of their own lives, to enhance their abilities and to live their purpose. Tying a gritty goal to your personal purpose increases your motivation and your grit exponentially. Simultaneously making progress toward the goal and the purpose increases self-satisfaction.

Extrinsic motivation is not as powerful as your intrinsic motivation. Daniel Pink describes it as "Do X Because Y." Examples of "Do X Because Y" are "You should get good grades so can go to a good college," "You should go to a good college so you can get a good job," and "You should do your job so you get paid." Eventually, the novelty of the "Y" loses its appeal. Yet, sometimes extrinsic motivation is the only way to get yourself going. Using extrinsic motivation to jump start your gritty journey or the growth of your grit is always an option.

WAYS TO UPGRADE YOUR MOTIVATION

There are hundreds of ways to upgrade your motivation. Writing your goal down, telling friends, refocusing the process, joining a group, hiring a coach, leveraging competition, using rewards or punishments, and using friends are the best tools that I have found to upgrade your motivation. Each tool has its time and place—each tool may only work with certain people and in certain situations. You have to figure out which tool works best for you.

One way to develop your motivation is to write your goal down and put it where you can see it. Want to write 1,000 words a day so you can put together a book? Then take out a pen and a Post-it Note®, write it down, and put it on your computer screen. Or take a dry erase marker and write it on your bathroom mirror. Putting your goal in writing and seeing it every day will energize your motivation.

Telling your goal to your family or close friends can be a way to upgrade your motivation. Want to earn your master of business administration (MBA)? Then tell your friends and family your goal is to take an executive MBA program at the local university at night over the next two years. The social accountability of telling the goal to your close circle, as well as the support you will get from the group, will energize your drive.

Like with forging stronger courage, changing your focus from winning or achieving something to focusing on learning or the process involved can boost your motivation in the same way. Focusing on enjoying the process enables you to be happy and have fun all the time, regardless of whether it works out. Having the focus be on the process is the only way to do intense, sustained, productive work over the long term and not be miserable.

An alternative method to develop your motivation around a gritty goal is to join a gritty group. Want to run a marathon? Then find the local runners' group that meets twice a week and join them for their runs. The power of the group will help energize your motivation to achieve your goal.

Hiring a teacher, coach, or mentor can upgrade your motivation. Want to learn how to play the piano? Then hire a piano teacher. The once-a-week lesson provides an incentive to practice, as well as providing you expert feedback to make you better. There is also a financial incentive—if you don't practice, you are just wasting your money. The power of a coach or teacher will help energize your drive to achieve your goal.

Another way to develop motivation is through competition. Say you have a goal to be more physically active. There are dozens of apps that provide a virtual leaderboard to track your progress and others. Personally, I like Strava for my endurance activities because every month Strava provides a virtual leaderboard for cycling distance. I can compare my miles on the bike to my friends who are also on Strava and ignite my motivation to ride more.

You can use a friend to develop your motivation. Want to walk 10,000 steps every day for a month? Set up a regular call, email, or text with a friend that wants to accomplish the same goal. Creating an external accountability system through your friend helps you track progress better and creates external pressure and responsibility to prevent you from taking a day off. The accountability and the motivation is stronger if you respect the friend.

Finally, rewards and punishments also help to develop motivation. I have a friend who lets herself buy a new bicycling kit or new running shoes if she meets a certain mileage goal for the month. When I accomplish something on my to-do list, I make an X in the box as my reward for completing the task. You have to determine which reward and which punishment works for you.

Use the eight tools to help you upgrade your motivation and grow your grit.

EXAMPLE

In July I joined the Trek Bicycles Century Challenge, which had a simple premise—ride 100 miles, 500 miles, or 1,000 miles during July to claim a small prize. To keep things interesting, Trek established a leaderboard on Strava. I had never ridden 1,000 miles in a month before. In fact, my record for a month was 764 miles in August 2019. Now, I know there are some incredible cyclists out there who have ridden a lot farther than I have, but I am proud to say that I rode 1,121 miles in July. My longest day was 70.6 miles and shortest was 12.1 miles. I rode every day during the month, averaging 36.16 miles per day. It required all of my perseverance to accomplish that achievement.

I fueled my motivation to pedal my bike as much as I could in July through almost all of the motivational tools. It was a tough challenge! I was committed to the process and riding my bike made me happy (except when I had saddle sores). It also made me healthier. I had the friends who were doing it and the leaderboard to track where my friends were in their quest. On the rough days when I was struggling to get out the door, I would text a friend and see if they wanted to ride. Finally, I knew I would receive a Trek coffee mug and a gold stem cap if I did 1,000 miles. This combination of intrinsic and extrinsic motivational tools grew my grit and pushed me to a new personal record.

OBSTACLE

One of the biggest challenges with motivation is figuring out what works for you. The journey to achieve one goal might rely heavily on intrinsic motivation while pursuing another goal only happens when it is fueled by extrinsic motivation. Recently, a corporate executive confessed to me that he was much grittier at work due to his intrinsic desire to be accountable to the team. It fueled him to accomplish goal after goal at work. On the other hand, he couldn't find the motivation to stick to his diet or his workout plan at home because he didn't feel the same accountability to himself or his family. I talked him through a couple of the ideas on intrinsic motivation, and he is back to eating healthy and losing a few pounds. Figuring out what works to upgrade your motivation takes time and practice.

CONCLUSION

Winning an NBA Championship or riding your bike 1,000 miles in a month both take grit and motivation. Whether you tie your goal to your purpose, write your goal down, tell the goal to a friend, focus on the learning or the process, join a group, hire a teacher, make the goal competitive, or use a friend for accountability, these tools can improve your motivation. Sometimes it takes more than one catalyst. Whatever it takes for you, go on the offensive and use intrinsic and extrinsic motivation to help you fuel your gritty growth and achieve your goal.

Chapter 8

THE MUNDANITY OF GRIT

"Real change, enduring change, happens one step at a time."
Supreme Court Justice Ruth Bader Ginsburg

RUTH BADER GINSBURG WAS JUST barely five feet tall, but she was a giant in the world of women's rights. Rejected by fourteen law firms after she graduated top in her classes from Harvard and Columbia Universities in the 1950s, Ginsburg's unbending resolve to smash glass ceilings was driven by first-hand experience. It was no small battle, but Ginsburg had grit: as a lawyer for the Women's Right Project at the American Civil Liberties Union (ACLU), she argued six landmark gender equality cases before the Supreme Court and won five of them. Her efforts ensured that that the Equal Protection Clause of the US Constitution's Fourteenth Amendment expanded to include women.

Due to her work at the ACLU, President Jimmy Carter appointed her as a judge to the US Court of Appeals for the District of Columbia in 1980. Over her thirteen years on the bench, Justice Ginsburg earned a reputation as a consensus builder and a moderate. In 1993,

President Bill Clinton nominated her to serve as the second woman on the US Supreme Court. During her twenty-seven years as a justice on the Supreme Court, she continued to advance equality including authoring the court's opinion in the *United States vs. Virginia,* which struck down the Virginia Military Institute's male-only admission policy. Later in her career, she was known for her passionate dissents and became a cultural icon as the "Notorious RBG."

Through her long, distinguished life, Ginsburg lived her personal purpose of expanding women's rights. She accumulated small wins over the course of her career that enabled her to keep up the momentum. She tenaciously battled cancer five times. She built her resilience by doing demanding physical fitness workouts in her eighties several days a week. She managed her fear of failure by saying, "I'm dejected, but only momentarily… But then you go on to the next challenge and you give it your all." For Justice Ruth Bader Ginsburg, grit was one of her habits.

HABITS

A habit is something that a person does often in a regular and repeated way. The US Army's approach to training soldiers is through building a compilation of habits. From the way to clean your weapon, to salute superior officers, to spit shine your shoes (fresh shoe polish, small circles with water, not spit), and to make your every day, one habit after another defines how people operate in the army. One habit I used every day since I was a lieutenant was to make a to-do list before I went to bed. Having the to-do list in my green notebook gave me a plan for work the next day, as well as an edge on the people who just showed up to work and reacted to whatever was thrown at them. Like the to-do list, many of the habits I learned in the US Army still resonate with me today—I still find myself waking up at 5:30 a.m. to get my exercise in every day.

It takes time to form a habit, whether it be good or bad. There is a popular misconception that it only takes twenty-one days to build a habit. However, recent research has shown that on average, it takes sixty-six days of repetition before a habit is formed or stopped. No matter how many days it takes to build a habit, you have to put in the work.

The New York Times journalist Charles Duhigg, in his book *The Power of Habit*, states that a simple three-part neurological loop is at the core of every habit: a cue, a routine, and a reward. For instance, if I lay my bike shoes and my kit out at night, they become my cue to go riding when I wake up in the morning. I take off and go for a twenty-five-mile ride down the Dragonfly Trail path by the river. When I finish, I get the reward of endorphins and a healthy feeling all day.

Grit is a Habit

Reward **Cue**

Habit

The Habit Cycle

Once you understand the loop, you can experiment with yourself to figure out why you have a current habit or how best to end a bad habit. For instance, if you have a bad habit, what is the trigger or cue? Most cues fall into five categories: *location, time, emotional state, other people, and immediately preceding action. Once you have categorized what the cue is, it* is worth examining what reward you receive. Changing the cue or the reward can change your habit.

A bad habit I have is drinking coffee in the afternoon, which then keeps me up at night. I find that on the days I pick up my daughter from school, I grab a cup of coffee for the drive at 2:30 p.m. So the cue is having to drive to pick her up, the action is drinking the cup of coffee, and the reward is alertness and the ability to do work while waiting in the carpool line. However, the downside is staring at the ceiling at 10:00 p.m. trying and failing to go to sleep. To change the bad habit, I can change the cue, the action, or the reward.

Or, if you are trying to create a habit, what works for you as a cue? What reward do you find compelling? Each of us is different; experimenting with different cues and rewards is helpful for understanding what creates a habit for you.

"The Mundanity of Excellence: An Ethnographic Report on Stratification of Olympic Swimmers" is an incredible article written by Daniel Chambliss. The author spent five years examining swimmers at every level from novice to Olympian to understand what makes swimmers excellent. He concludes that "Excellence is mundane. Superlative performance is really a confluence of dozens of small skills or activities, each one learned or stumbled upon, which have been carefully drilled into habit and then fitted together into a synthesized whole."

Like excellence, grit is a habit and is built upon the mundane. There are dozens of small skills and activities that each must be mastered, drilled into a habit, and then combined and synchronized into a whole that enable us to have grit and accomplish a gritty goal. I have found that to pursue and achieve a long-term goal, one must improve and enhance their perseverance, their resilience, their courage to deal with the fear of failure, and their motivation. Although each of the tasks are small in themselves, improving each until mastery is achieved enables you to gradually achieve your goal. In short, it's the little things that count.

This idea seems daunting. At the end of the movie *The Martian*, after spending 560 days alone on Mars before his rescue, Mark Watney (the astronaut played by Matt Damon) talks to a new bunch of astronauts. He tells them "At some point, everything's gonna go south on you ... everything's going to go south and you're going to say, this is it. This is how I end. Now you can either accept that, or you can get to work. That's all it is. You just begin. You do the math. You solve one problem ... and you solve the next one ... and then the next. And If you solve enough problems, you get to come home." This idea of breaking the problem down and working small problems is not just in the movies, it is part of NASA's culture too. This was clear during the Apollo 13 near-disaster. The team on the ground in Houston and in space broke the overarching problem down into little ones. The team then worked each one until the crew was home safely.

Now, we aren't faced with the problem of how to survive on Mars by ourselves for over a year, but the concept is the same. Whether you want to run a marathon, earn an MBA, or balance your checkbook every month, you must break your gritty problem down into parts. Then figure out ways to optimize and habitualize elements of your perseverance, your resilience, your courage, and your motivation. Together, the small enhancements make the journey more manageable. You may also need to figure out things that you are currently doing that must be abandoned so you have the bandwidth to do the new things necessary to accomplish your gritty goal.

Growing your grit is mundane. It isn't easy, but like Justice Ginsberg said, "It happens one step at a time." Go on the offensive and habitualize your small elements of grit so you can thrive and can accomplish your long-term goal.

Chapter 9

THE GRIT CRUCIBLE—THE US ARMY'S RANGER SCHOOL

"Compared to Ranger School, combat was easy."

Colonel Robert "Tex" Turner, US Army Ranger

MANY GRITTY PEOPLE HAVE AN experience, or crucible, that helped grow their personal grit. It might have happened trying to climb a mountain, being part of a sports team, earning a doctorate, or finishing an Ironman. One of my grit crucibles was the US Army's Ranger School. Like with Tex Turner, the grit I developed in Ranger School was critical to my actions in combat a decade later.

EGLIN AIR FORCE BASE, FLORIDA

It was a dark night in the panhandle of Florida in February 1994. A little over half the class that had started with me was still here. My dirty uniform hung loosely on my emaciated body. The skin on my hands had started to peel off from the constant exposure to water and cold weather. The pungent smell of sweat was everywhere. Exhaustion, hunger, stress, and exertion had stripped away our facades. I had spent the last ten days carrying seventy-five pounds on my back, trudging miles each day in the cypress-studded swamps. Within striking distance of the end of my months-long ordeal to earn the Ranger Tab, I knew I had fallen short. I had failed to meet the standard and receive a "Go" from a Ranger instructor during my two opportunities leading a patrol during the Florida phase of Ranger School. Each time I was in a leadership role was a disaster—people fell asleep during an ambush, weapons didn't work, and we were uncoordinated.

The cadre asked me if I wanted to recycle (repeat the Florida phase). I thought to myself, did I want to spend another two weeks slogging through the swamps? Could my body take it? Could I actually achieve a "Go" in a leadership position? Mulling it over, I said "Yes. I want to give it another shot." I took the recycle opportunity because I saw myself as someone who doesn't quit and because, for the last four years, my heroes, like Dave Lamm and Guy LoFaro, wore the Ranger Tab. I took it because I knew some of my friends had just earned the Ranger Tab and because I had told my friends and family that I was going to get my Ranger Tab. I took it because I had perseverance, resilience, and grit.

After a four-day break, the next Ranger class arrived at the camp and started training. I was assigned to a new squad, and we got to work bonding and developing our standard operating procedures. After a parachute jump, we plunged back into the swamps full of cypress trees and alligators. I got my "Go" on my first patrol and proudly pinned on my Ranger Tab in a ceremony a few days later at Fort Benning, Georgia. The US Army's Ranger School put me out of my comfort zone for over two months where I built my resilience, enhanced my perseverance, found my motivation, and grew my grit by daily overcoming adversity.

THE US ARMY RANGER SCHOOL

In addition to attending and graduating from Ranger School, I led the Airborne and Ranger Training Brigade, which runs Ranger School, from 2014–2016. Over the two years, more than 7,000 students attempted the course and just over 3,000 earned the Ranger Tab. Overseeing the army's premier small unit leadership school was challenging to say the least. Every day of training was high risk. Behind the scenes, the Ranger Instructors (Ranger-qualified, experienced noncommissioned officers) worked hard to ensure the students were held to high standards; developed the student's leadership, tactics, and grit; and maintained an invisible safety net so the training could be conducted safely.

Grit is "the will to persevere to achieve long-term goals," and Ranger School is a grit crucible. As the sign at the front gate says, Ranger School is NOT FOR THE WEAK OR FAINTHEARTED. Over its sixty-one days, the average student survives on three hours of sleep and loses twenty pounds of weight due to the high physical demands of carrying 100-plus pounds of gear every day. Since 1952, it has pushed its students' boundaries by showing them that they can move further and fight harder than they ever thought. The course weeds out those lacking grit—over the years only 40 to 50 percent of those that walk through its gates graduate and earn the Ranger Tab.

In spite of the adversity, over the years 90,000 people have graduated and earned the Ranger Tab. Famous Ranger graduates include retired General David H. Petraeus, singer and actor Kris Kristofferson, retired General and former Secretary of State Colin Powell, Medal of Honor recipient and Best Ranger Competition winner Sergeant Major Thomas Payne, Medal of Honor recipient Colonel Ralph Puckett, and former Federal Bureau of Investigation Director Robert Mueller.

Ranger School consists of four phases. The first phase, or Ranger Assessment phase, occurs at Fort Benning, Georgia. Ranger students must successfully pass a physical fitness test, a swim test, a land navigation test, a basic soldier skills test, and a foot march. Although the students are told the standards for all the tests they take the first week, the vast majority of the attrition in the school still happens in the first four days.

The second phase of Ranger School is the Benning phase. Students are required to plan and conduct six days of patrols in the rolling hills of south-central Georgia. During each patrol, different students are placed in leadership roles and evaluated on their performance by a Ranger instructor. At the end of the six days of patrols, small units conduct peer evaluations of each other, as a 360-degree evaluation tool. To pass the Benning phase, the student must have received a "Go" on a patrol while in a leadership position and have been ranked in the top 75 percent of their unit by their peers. Students who fail either of those benchmarks are offered the opportunity to repeat the phase. Failing either patrols or peers twice in the same phase results in the student being dropped from the course.

The third phase of Ranger School is the Mountain phase, which occurs in the North Georgia mountains near Dahlonega, Georgia. Students must pass a knots test and are introduced to basic military mountaineering at Mount Yonah. Students then plan and conduct ten days of patrols, raids, and ambushes in the rugged mountains near the Appalachian Trail. During each patrol, students are placed in leadership roles and evaluated on their performance by a Ranger instructor. At the end of the ten days of patrols, small units conduct peer evaluations of each other. The same rules for pass and fail in the Benning phase apply to the Mountain phase.

The fourth phase of Ranger School is the Swamp phase, which occurs in the swamps near Eglin Air Force Base, Florida. After a short introduction to Florida reptiles, small boat operations, and operating in a coastal swamp, students then plan and conduct ten days of patrols, raids, and ambushes, where they are, again, placed in leadership roles and evaluated by Ranger instructors. They are also judged by their peers. The same standards apply to pass the Swamp phase.

Due to the gritty nature of Ranger School, most Ranger students recycle at least one phase before graduating. Some exceptionally gritty Ranger students have had the opportunity to do three follow-on phases. Despite being recycled, Ranger students must rely on their resilience to bounce back, learn from their mistakes, and pass a patrol to move on. As one sergeant major confessed, "I quit Ranger School every day, I just didn't have the guts to tell anyone."

GRIT CRUCIBLE

Most students who come to Fort Benning to test themselves at Ranger School come in with some measure of grit. The students have graduated high school, been part of a sports team, worked a part-time job, graduated college, passed several US Army schools, or completed some combination of these. They certainly distinguished themselves from their peers in their unit, have trained themselves to a high degree of physical fitness, and may have even passed a pre-Ranger course. But every student's grit is grown by their experience at the school.

Ranger School enhanced the grit of its students through a multidimensional approach. First, students must develop grit at the most basic level by learning to deal with being hungry, tired, and constantly performing extreme physical activities. Second, the student's grit is tested and grown while learning how to be a follower through the peer evaluations and figuring out how to be value-added to the team. Whether that is by helping develop the plan, going to get water for the group, or carrying the seventeen-pound machine gun, the group respects those who contribute. Failing to help and focusing on oneself at the expense of the team result in a poor 360-degree evaluation. Ranger students must also develop grit as leaders. When put into a leadership role, they must find ways to motivate and inspire their cold, wet, hungry, and exhausted teammates. As a leader, there are few things harder than keeping a group of Ranger students awake in an ambush line in the mountains of Georgia in February at 1:00 a.m.

For both followers and leaders, Ranger School develops perseverance, resilience, courage to deal with the fear of failure, and motivation. While climbing Denali, running a marathon, graduating from college, or writing a book are all worthy grit crucibles, the US Army's multidimensional approach to developing personal grit at Ranger School sets it apart from other experiences as a true grit crucible.

During my time leading the ARTB, I oversaw the gender integration of Ranger School. Nineteen women started the course, and three earned their Ranger Tabs. The nineteen women who showed up on April 20, 2015 demonstrated grit by volunteering to meet the standards of a tough course, while breaking a glass ceiling. The first three women graduates—Kristen Griest, Shaye Haver, and Lisa Jaster—demonstrated extreme grit. As Kristen Griest said, "I think I had like three of the hardest days of my life each week at Ranger School." Yet she persevered and kept putting one foot in front of the other until she earned the Ranger Tab. Ranger School graduates—both women and men—have grit.

WHAT'S YOUR RANGER SCHOOL?

Only 3,500 students attend the crucible of Ranger School each year. But the concept that every person needs a crucible to help develop your grit can apply to anyone. Want to be a better person, leader, family member, and friend? Take on a tough, gritty challenge.

Grit crucibles can come in all shapes and sizes. Over the past several years, I have taken on the challenge of racing a half-Ironman, climbing Currahee Mountain, and now writing a book. You may decide to run a marathon, go back to school to get a master's degree, earn your real estate license, learn a new language, or climb Mount Kilimanjaro. Whatever it is for you, finding a gritty crucible that builds your perseverance, enhances your courage, creates resilience, and develops your motivation can be your personal Ranger School. Find your personal Ranger School and grow your personal grit.

Chapter 10

PERSONAL GRIT CHECKLIST

"The backbone of success is ... hard work, determination, good planning, and perseverance."

Mia Hamm, Olympic soccer player

MIA HAMM IS A SOCCER icon who played forward for the US women's national team from 1987 to 2004. She was instrumental in the University of North Carolina winning four consecutive NCAA Division I Women's Soccer Championship titles, and the US national team winning two Olympic gold medals and two Women's World Cup titles. When she retired, she held the record for most international goals scored with 158. Hamm was an incredibly strong, tough, competitive, selfless, and creative athlete. Renowned for her intense two-a-day training in the gym and on the field, she embraced the philosophy that "consistency is the most important but neglected part of fitness."

Most people aren't as gritty as Mia Hamm, though. Mia Hamm defined her personal purpose, established goals, honed her perseverance, and built her courage, resilience, and motivation to create grit and take herself and her team to the highest levels. Figuring out where to start developing your personal grit is a huge challenge for many people. A checklist can help the process.

CHECKLISTS

Checklists are a list of items required, things to be done, or points to be considered, and are often used as a reminder. They are simple but powerful tools used by pilots, doctors, astronauts, construction workers, and the military to handle complex, nonroutine problems. Checklists help people balance innovation and discipline, art and science, specialized talents, and group collaboration. Michael Collins, one of the three Apollo 11 crew members who went to the moon, referred to the astronauts' ubiquitous checklists as "the fourth crew member."

Checklists weren't always so widespread. In 1935 at Wright Field in Ohio, the Army Air Corps hosted a fly-off between two long-range bombers: the Douglas Aircraft Company's B-18, a two-engine bomber, and the Boeing B-17, a four-engine, cutting-edge aircraft with controllable pitch propellers, retractable landing gear, flaps, and an average speed of 232 miles per hour. During the fly-off, the B-17 crashed immediately after takeoff. Subsequently, the Army Air Corps selected Douglas for the contract to produce 200 B-18 bombers.

Despite its crash, the Army Air Corps still wanted the B-17. An investigation determined that the airplane crashed due to pilot error, not the aircraft's size or complexity. To avoid another accident, Air Corps personnel developed checklists the crew would follow for takeoff, flight, before landing, and after landing to minimize the opportunity for future human error. Until this time, the checklist had been used in aviation, but infrequently. It took the crash of the B-17, as well as the development of an extremely complex airplane, to institutionalize the use of checklists throughout the aviation world. Once the checklists were implemented, Boeing went on to produce over 12,000 B-17s. The Boeing Flying Fortresses were the workhorse of the bombing campaign against Germany in World War II.

The crash of the B-17 was the catalyst for checklists to become commonplace in aviation. In addition to pilots, checklists are used today by doctors in operating rooms to reduce the risk of infection, construction workers to build complex buildings, and soldiers to make sure their vehicles operate correctly. Checklists take the pressure off people trying to remember all the necessary steps to make complex systems work effectively as well as freeing bandwidth for the operators to think about more challenging tasks.

Over the last nine decades, checklists have been refined and improved. Boeing and Airbus both have departments dedicated to building checklists to support all their aircraft. Checklists fall into three categories: they help people and organizations perform routine procedures better, prepare better, or problem-solve better. The best checklists are only one page long and only hit the most important steps. Interestingly, they include opportunities for the group or team to pause and communicate.

I love checklists. I make a checklist every night for the things that I need to get done the next day. This helps keep me focused on the pursuit of my long-term goals. They help me stay gritty. My roommate from West Point, Andrew Hyatt, laminated checklists so he could use them over and over.

Because checklists are so powerful, I have provided a procedural checklist to help you better handle the complex system of growing your grit. Use it to decrease uncertainty and avoid mistakes. Use it to help you better follow the process, develop your purpose, design a goal, enhance your perseverance, and upgrade your motivation as you grow your personal grit and accomplish amazing things.

THE PERSONAL GRIT CHECKLIST

- ☐ At the beginning:
    - Take stock of your level of grit by using the Grit Quiz in Chapter 1.
    - Examine your personal purpose. Do the exercise in Chapter 2 to solidify your understanding of your core values and your personal purpose.
    - Develop your goal or goals. Make sure the goal uses the mnemonic device SMART, break down the steps to achieve your goal, and block time on your calendar to work toward your goal. Write your goal down where you can see it daily (on your mirror or near your computer). Refer to Chapter 3 if you need extra help.
    - Develop your courage. List your fears, reframe your definition of success and failure, and focus on all the things you will be learning along the way. Refer to Chapter 6 if you need additional ideas.
- ☐ Pause and communicate: Talk to close friends and family about your purpose, goals, and fears.
- ☐ Daily: Build your perseverance and momentum. Start and maintain a streak or celebrate your small wins. Refer to Chapter 4 if you need more ideas.
- ☐ Daily: Resilience. Make sure you are taking care of yourself daily to optimize your resilience. Ensure you are sleeping well, eating healthy, working out daily (even if only ten minutes), and practicing mindfulness. Refer to Chapter 5 if you need help.
- ☐ Daily: Revisit your motivation. Make sure you are continuing to fuel your grit. Refer to Chapter 7 if you need more ideas.
- ☐ Monthly: Take stock of where you were, what you've accomplished so far, where you are, and where you are going.

- ☐ Pause and communicate: Talk to close friends and family about how you are making progress toward your goal, as well as your successes and your struggles.
- ☐ Quarterly:
  - Goal: Take stock of where you were, what you've accomplished, where you are, and where you are going. Then ask yourself if it is still the right goal.
  - Perseverance: Make sure you are maintaining your streak or are starting one. Find what works to keep it going.
  - Habits: Revisit your habits. Make sure your habits are getting you closer to your goal. Eliminate habits that are inhibiting your pursuit of your goal.
- ☐ Pause and communicate: Talk to close friends and family about your goal, streaks, habits, successes, and struggles.

If you reach your goal, pause, celebrate, and communicate. Then go back to the top and start a new, grittier journey.

If you don't reach your goal in twelve months, go back to the top and use the annual exercise to reexamine your purpose and goal. If it is still what you want to do, get after it. If not, start a new gritty journey.

CONCLUSION

It's not enough to just read about and contemplate your grit. Take this book, reread the previous ten chapters, and develop a plan to build your personal grit. Understand your personal purpose, select a goal, and get to work. If you are stuck, use the checklist to help get you going.

But developing your personal grit is just the start. Understanding how to grow your personal grit is important to understanding yourself and developing insights into how your family, your friends, your coworkers, and even your adversaries grow their grit. Do your family, friends, coworkers, and adversaries have grit? Are they building their grit? Or is their grit atrophying?

Organizational grit is different than personal grit. It is not just the sum of everyone's individual grit. Whether you are a parent, a teacher, a coach, a leader, an executive, or a director, you are probably struggling with how to grow your group into a gritty organization. The next eight chapters will help you develop a method to grow grit in an organization.

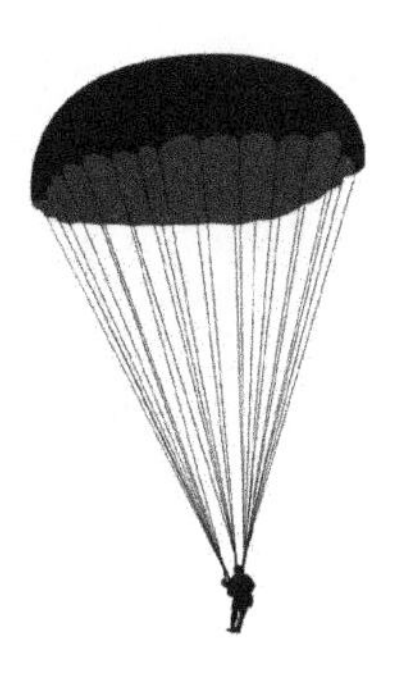

SECTION II

GROW YOUR ORGANIZATION'S GRIT

Chapter 11

ORGANIZATIONAL GRIT

"I've always thought of problems as challenges, and this one wasn't any different. ... But I didn't dwell on my disappointment. The challenge at hand was simple enough to figure out: I had to pick myself up, do it all over again, only even better this time."

Sam Walton, founder of Walmart

SAM WALTON GREW UP IN Missouri during the Great Depression. After earning his Eagle Scout and graduating from the University of Missouri, he joined the army during World War II. When the war ended, he took his family to Newport, Arkansas and bought a Ben Franklin convenience store. The store was wildly successful, but Walton lost the store when his lease expired. Drawing on the lesson and his grit, he opened a new store in Bentonville, Arkansas in 1950. He slowly grew his Ben Franklin stores until he had a chain of fifteen across three states.

In 1962, Walton decided to go out on his own and opened the first Walmart in Rogers, Arkansas. He focused his efforts on building clean, well-run stores in small towns that leveraged buying in volume and efficient logistics to provide low prices to the customer every day. He was an innovator too—he was one of the first retailers to embrace self-service, discounting, and using computers to help control inventory. By focusing on small towns, he was able to dominate the market, often running the mom-and-pop stores, as well as other chains stores (Ben Franklin, Western Auto, Sears, and Kmart) out of business.

The company went public in 1970 and steadily expanded. Walton was everywhere providing leadership and energy—visiting stores, talking to customers, listening to associates, and inspiring managers. Walmart had a purpose of providing low prices and great service, followed a plan of how to get there, and developed a persistent culture where the associates were as committed as Walton because they had ownership in the success of the store. In short, Walmart, under Sam Walton, had organizational grit. The long-term focus paid off—when Sam Walton died, Walmart had 1,960 stores, 380,000 employees, and sales of $50 billion in 1992.

From 2001 to 2014, the McKinsey Institute studied companies that focused on short-term goals and those that focused on long-term goals. Interestingly, the revenue of long-term-focused firms cumulatively grew on average 47 percent more than the revenue of the short-term-focused firms, and, similarly, the earnings of firms with a long-term focus grew 36 percent more than the firms with a short-term focus. So, if long-term-focused firms, like Walmart, perform better, why don't all companies focus on the long-term? One of the factors possessed by the organizations focused on the long-term is organizational grit. The firms with short-term focus don't have it or don't have as much of it.

ORGANIZATIONAL GRIT

While groups are a collection of people, organizational grit is different than just the sum of each member of the group's individual grit. Gritty people do help to form gritty organizations, but organizational grit is different. Organizational grit is better defined as "the group's will to persevere to achieve long-term goals."

After looking at sports teams, the units I was part of in the army, corporate examples, companies I've worked with, and other examples, I have developed a theory on the formation of organizational grit. I find that organizational grit is grown through the following ways.

- Providing the team a purpose.
- Giving the group a goal and a plan of how to get there.
- Providing the organization a scoreboard that tracks the progress.
- Modeling and growing an organizational culture that values daily small wins ("every day a little better"), self-discipline, and resiliency.
- Developing trust in the team that is grown through shared experiences and hardships.

The most important (but often hidden) element behind the growth of organizational grit is leadership. Leaders, like Sam Walton, help inculcate grit in their organizations. Throughout the process, leaders in these organizations I examined demonstrated grit and led by example, using their position to instill determination, energy, and leadership within each of their followers.

What is Organizational Grit?

The group's will to persevere to achieve long term goals

Organizational Grit

Organizational grit is present in sports, the military, nonprofits, and businesses. It isn't easy to achieve. There is no magic bullet. Although all groups desire it, some can grow it, and some can't. The groups that have organizational grit gain a competitive advantage over their peers, like Walmart. Here are three examples of other gritty organizations.

ORGANIZATIONAL GRIT IN SPORTS

In sports, there are thousands of stories of teams that have more organizational grit than talent and are able to beat better teams. The 1990–1994 Buffalo Bills were an exceptionally gritty team. Coach Marv Levy forged a resilient team behind quarterback Jim Kelley that was able to make it to the Super Bowl four years in a row. The Bills, unfortunately, lost all four Super Bowls. Think about the grit required every year, after losing the Super Bowl, to get back to the biggest game in professional football. It is staggering to think about thirty years later. Levy was a master at motivating the team.

The Bills' grit and perseverance were epitomized by Don Beebe, one of their wide receivers. During Super Bowl XXVII (1993), between the Buffalo Bills and the Dallas Cowboys, Beebe made a play that I will never forget. In the fourth quarter, with the Bills behind by thirty-five points, the Bills' quarterback, Frank Reich, was sacked. The ball came free, and the Cowboys' defensive tackle, Leon Lett, scooped the ball up and started running sixty yards to the end zone. Lett started celebrating at the ten-yard line. A sprinting Don Beebe chased Lett down and knocked the ball out of his hands, right before the goal line. The ball went out of the end zone, and it was ruled a touchback. Buffalo got the ball back on the twenty-yard line.

I'm not even a fan of the Buffalo Bills, but their grit was undeniable. Getting to the Super Bowl, losing, and fighting your way back next year takes true grit. Hustling even when the game was out of reach typified the grit of the players on the Buffalo Bills. The Bills' purpose, culture, and bonds between teammates got them to the championship game four years in a row.

ORGANIZATIONAL GRIT IN BUSINESS

When looking at other examples of gritty corporate entities like Walmart, another great example is the Lego Group, a privately held Danish company. The Lego Group has been making interlocking plastic toy bricks since 1949. Yet in 2003, the company was in trouble—losing money and $800 million in debt.

Vig Knudstorp, a thirty-six-year-old former consultant from McKinsey, was brought in to turn the company around. Knudstorp first focused on working with the leaders and employees to rediscover Lego's purpose. After much deliberation, they went with "Inspire and Develop the Builders of Tomorrow." Then he developed a strategy that enabled them to live that purpose, as well as rebuild the company, brick by brick. Lego got rid of products that they had no expertise in, slashed inventory, reconnected with fans, and created new products marketed to young girls. In addition, the shared experience of overcoming near bankruptcy built powerful bonds in the company.

The turnaround didn't happen overnight. Relentlessly, year after year, Lego's organizational grit slowly reestablished it as a leader in the toy market. The results speak for themselves—in 2015, the privately owned company overtook Ferrari to become the world's most powerful brand with a profit of $886 million. Purpose, strategy, and strong bonds between employees turned things around for the Lego Group.

ORGANIZATIONAL GRIT AT THE NATIONAL LEVEL

British Prime Minister Winston Churchill was a man of action—as a cavalry officer in three colonial wars, battalion commander on the Western Front in World War I, author of forty books, recipient of the Nobel Prize for literature, painter, reporter, airplane pilot, farmer, bricklayer, and a member of Parliament. His government positions included: Colonial Undersecretary and Secretary, President of the Board of Trade, Home Secretary, two-time First Lord of the Admiralty, Minister of Munitions, Chancellor of the Exchequer, and two-time Prime Minister twice. More importantly he was a gritty leader—of small military units as an officer, of his party in Parliament, of his departments in the executive branch of the British government, and of the country as prime minister.

During the dark days of 1940, Prime Minister Churchill provided the British people with purpose and grit at the national level when the odds seemed stacked against them. On May 13, 1940, in the "Blood, Toil, Tears, and Sweat" speech to a packed House of Commons, Churchill gave one of the world's greatest purpose statements:

> You ask, what is our policy? I can say: It is to wage war, by sea, land, and air, with all our might and with all the strength that God can give us; to wage war against a monstrous tyranny, never surpassed in the dark, lamentable catalogue of human crime. That is our policy. You ask, what is our aim? I can answer in one word: It is victory, victory at all costs, victory in spite of all terror, victory, however long and hard the road may be; for without victory, there is no survival. Let that be realized; no survival for the British Empire, no survival for all that the British Empire has stood for, no survival for the urge and impulse of the ages, that mankind will move forward towards its goal.

This speech provided a goal, a purpose, alignment, organizational grit, and resilience for the British people and government to use against Nazi Germany. Even Churchill acknowledged the impact, saying, "The nation ... had the lion's heart. I had the luck to be called upon to give the roar." The British used their organizational grit to help turn the tide and defeat the Axis Powers in World War II.

Walmart, the Buffalo Bills, the Lego Group, and the British people during World War II all had grit. Each group leveraged that grit and their long-term focus to gain a competitive advantage over their adversaries. You can apply the same concepts to your organization, enhance its grit, and beat your competitors.

DUNBAR'S NUMBER

In the 1990s, Robin Dunbar, a British anthropologist, examined historic literature for information on twenty-one different hunter-gather societies, the Roman army, and Hutterite religious settlements. He learned the size of these diverse groups throughout history kept being right around 150 people. Combining that information with research on primate and human brains, he concluded that humans had a cognitive limit of 150 people that they can maintain stable social relationships with.

It is sometimes difficult to see grit in larger organizations due in part to Dunbar's number. Most sports teams, small military units such as platoons and companies, and small businesses have fewer than 150 people. These groups are often characterized as gritty because it is easier to see the social connections between the members.

For centuries, military organizations have been built around Dunbar's number. After the Marian reforms in 107 BCE that transformed the Roman army from a semiprofessional militia to a professional fighting force, a subdivision called centuries, comprised of eighty men, became the backbone of the Roman legions. With these centuries, Rome built an empire. Dunbar says that the 150-manlimit enables "orders ... [to be] implemented and unruly behavior controlled on the basis of personal loyalties and man-to-man contacts." With larger groups, this is impossible.

I found this true in the modern US Army, too. Platoons (approximately forty people) and companies (approximately 150 people) shared alignment, social bonds, and teamwork. In both formations, I, as the leader, was able to know each member of the team, their background, their strengths, and the best way to lead them. The grittiest organization I have been part of was C Company, 3rd Battalion, 504th Parachute Infantry Regiment (PIR) because of its purpose, culture, and bonds between the paratroopers. When I moved up to work and lead a battalion (approximately 670 people) and a brigade (approximately 1,500 people) I didn't know everyone in the group. It became tougher to see the grit in the entire organization and understand how gritty we were or weren't. But if I looked at the companies, it was easy to see which ones were gritty and which ones weren't.

In his book *The Tipping Point*, Malcolm Gladwell also discusses Dunbar's number. W. L. Gore and Associates, known for the Gore-Tex brand, is a $3.8 billion in revenue per year company with 10,500 employees and has been ranked as one of the top 100 Best Companies to Work For by *Fortune Magazine* for the past three decades. Gladwell uses it as an example of Dunbar's number in action. Gore discovered that social problems arose if more than 150 employees were working together in one building. More importantly, 150 people was the largest organization that could maintain alignment and "genuine social relationship" between all members of the team. To keep the advantages of 150 people organizations, Gore built buildings that had a limit of 150 employees and only 150 parking spaces. When the parking spaces were filled, the company would build another 150-employee building.

Whether you are in a hunter-gather society, a military unit, a sports team, or a corporation, Dunbar's number governs the number of social relationships a person can maintain. It also can be used as a benchmark to support an organization's desire to grow its grit because it is easier to see the social connections in any group with less than 150 people. Because a sports team is smaller than Dunbar's number, reporters can see the social connections on the team and write about the connections. Fans can see the connections between the owner, the head coach, the assistant coaches, the quarterback, the running backs, the wide receivers, and the linemen. And players can more easily connect with each other, bond over shared experiences and goals, and ultimately work more effectively together. Sports teams are characterized as gritty because they are a small enough organization that people can recognize, organize, remember, and understand the social connections between the team members and coaches.

ORGANIZATIONAL GRIT ASSESSMENT

Before trying to cultivate or sustain organizational grit, it is worth examining where the team's grit is today. Determining your group's level of grit singlehandedly never works well. Instead, it must be a team effort. It's critical to bring the group together and discuss everyone's perspective of where your grit is and ideas about where they would like to be. If the whole group is participating and understanding the group's current and desired future grit, it is much easier to get the commitment needed to make the changes necessary to grow.

I find that this exercise works best in a room with a large wall and dozens of Post-it Notes for every participant. Read through the questions below and select the ones that will stimulate the most discussion. Then write the questions on pieces of paper and put them on the wall where everyone can see them. Have each participant write their answer to each question on the Post-it Note, and after twenty minutes have everyone go up to the wall and put their Post-it Note underneath the corresponding question. Have a facilitator (not the leader) take the group through a discussion of the answers to each question. The answers and the discussion should provide a good perspective on the status of the team's grit.

Here are eighteen questions to help stimulate the discussion. I recommend only picking the ten most relevant to your group's situation. Or develop your own. But use the questions to ignite a meaningful discussion about where the organization's grit is today.

- Without looking it up, what is our organization's purpose or our *why*? (If you don't have one there is an exercise in Chapter 12 to help you start making one.)
- Did we have a stretch goal last year?
- Did we achieve our stretch goal last year?
- What were our top five goals last year?

- Did we achieve our top five goals from last year?
- What was our biggest failure last year?
- How did we rebound from the failure?
- What was our biggest obstacle last year?
- How did we handle it (or what was our approach) when we encountered the obstacle?
- What are our values? Is grit one of them?
- What division, section, or group is our grittiest?
- What division, section, or group is our most fainthearted (the opposite of gritty)?
- What division, section, or group has the best teamwork?
- What division, section, or group is our most dysfunctional?
- What leader is our grittiest? How gritty is his or her group?
- What leader is our most fainthearted? How gritty is his or her group?
- What person is our grittiest? How gritty is the group he or she is part of?
- What person is our most fainthearted? How gritty is the group he or she is part of?

When the discussion is over, reflect on the responses, and write a paragraph assessment of where your group's grit is today. Write a second paragraph about where you would like it to be. If you were Marv Levy, the Buffalo Bills' head coach in 1993, an assessment might look like this:

> *Last year, the 1992–1993 Buffalo Bills failed to win Super Bowl XXVII, losing to the Cowboys 52–17. We went 11–5 in the regular season and qualified for the playoffs via the wildcard. Our biggest obstacle was the Wildcard Playoff game against the Houston Oilers. Down 31–3, Frank Reich, our backup quarterback, led us on a 35–3 run*

> *in the second half, which tied the game. Steve Christie kicked a field goal in overtime to win it. The game is known as "The Comeback." Our offense was our grittiest department with the best rushing offense in the NFL and the third best offense overall. The defense was our most fainthearted department, ranking fourteenth overall—it was great against the run, not so great against the pass. Of course, our grittiest person is Don Beebe, a wide receiver, due to his play throughout the season and in the post-season.*
>
> *Next year, our purpose is to be the best team in the NFL and win the Super Bowl. Two goals are to win our division and get homefield advantage in the playoffs. We must maintain our offense at the same high level while increasing the performance and grit of our defense. We are looking to draft one or two gritty, talented people to help shore up the defense.*

Share the paragraphs with the leadership team. See what works, what doesn't, and what gets the team excited. Then refine it. When you're finally satisfied with it (no more than a week after the discussion), publish it to the entire organization. At every opportunity over the next several months (such as meetings, one-on-ones, and discussions), prioritize communicating the findings so that all the members of the organization are on the same page. Even when you're tired of hearing it, communicate it some more. Everyone needs to know where your team's grit is and where you are committing to going.

OBSTACLE

One of the biggest challenges in growing and sustaining organizational grit is determining if grit is worth pursuing. In any organization, there are dozens of systems and processes that all compete for limited bandwidth, time, and attention. The organizational grit process discussed in the next six chapters combines growing grit with developing your group's purpose, planning, culture, teams, and leadership. As you are debating whether to spend the time on growing your group's grit, remember that the organizations that focus on the long-term have a competitive advantage over their short-term peers.

CONCLUSION

A purpose, a goal and a plan, a scoreboard, a gritty culture, and building trust in the team helped turn the Buffalo Bills, the Lego Group, and the British people during World War II into gritty organizations. Walmart's grit, and its focus on selling for less in small rural markets, gave it a leg up on the competition and enabled it to become the world's biggest retailer. The next six chapters will break down each part of grit, as well as give you some great ideas on how to build and maintain "the group's will to persevere to achieve long-term goals." It's not simple or easy to cultivate organizational grit. If it were easy, every organization would be gritty. After looking at each part, the organizational grit blueprint in Chapter 18 combines all the information together into a holistic approach that has worked for other organizations.

Chapter 12

CULTIVATE YOUR ORGANIZATION'S PURPOSE

"When you're surrounded by people who share a passionate commitment around a common purpose, everything is possible."

Howard Schultz, CEO, Starbucks

FOUNDED AS A COFFEE SHOP in Seattle in 1971, the Starbucks Corporation grew to more than 16,000 locations in 2007. Late that year, as the financial crisis and recession approached, Starbucks had lost its purpose. Revenue was flat at $9.8 Billion. The focus on growth had overshadowed that stores were attracting fewer customers, products other than coffee distracted customers and weren't selling, the supply chain had issues, and the point-of-sale infrastructure was antiquated.

To overcome these huge challenges, Howard Schulz, who served as Starbucks chief executive officer from 1986 to 2000, was brought back to help the company find its soul. In March 2008, he brought the leadership team together in Seattle to rediscover their company's purpose. After deep thought, Starbucks crafted a purpose statement and dedicated themselves "to inspire and nurture the human spirit—one person, one cup and one neighborhood at a time." They didn't stop there. Their first order of business was to make sure they were the undisputed authority in coffee. A new semiautomatic espresso machine, the new Pike Place Roast, and having each store grind beans several times a day helped them get back to the fundamentals. Second, Schultz closed the doors of every Starbucks, retrained every employee through a video, and recommitted the company to inspiring and nurturing the human spirit. The company lost $60 million in revenue in one day for that closing, but the refocus on purpose more than made up for the loss by developing deeper connections with the company's loyal customers. Finally, Schultz wanted every old and new store's ambience, as well as its sights, sounds, smells, and employees, to spotlight their great coffee and bring people together.

Schultz spent a lot of time over the next two years communicating the purpose to his leaders, his board, and the hundreds of thousands of Starbucks employees. They worked hard to make sure the company embodied the purpose. The focus on the purpose in each and every store got Starbucks back on track, fixed problems, and enabled domestic and global expansion. Shultz's focus on purpose worked—Starbucks had $22.3 billion in revenue and $2.8 billion in profits in 2017, Shultz's final year as CEO.

PURPOSE VS. VISION VS. MISSION STATEMENTS

Organizations routinely have statements that describe their purpose, vision, and mission. Although these statements may make sense in the C-Suite, the differences in each of the statements can cause confusion within the team when they filter down to the lower levels of the organization. It helps to remember the definitions of these terms.

- Purpose Statement: The *why* for your company or your organization.
- Vision Statement: What your organization will look like in the future. It provides the direction and focus for the next several years so the organization can achieve the vision.
- Mission Statement: What the organization does and who it does the work for.

RaceTrac Petroleum is a third-generation, family-owned company headquartered in Atlanta. It owns and operates more than 670 convenience stores and gas stations across the southeast United States. Their revenue was estimated at $11 billion in 2019. They have all three statements.

- Purpose: To make people's lives simpler and more enjoyable.
- Vision: Become the convenience store of choice.
- Mission Statement: Place our people first, ensure open honest communications, and always provide tasty food, competitive prices, and friendly service.

ORGANIZATIONAL PURPOSE STATEMENT

Of course, I favor the purpose statement because it plays such an important role in the leader's intent, shaping your organizational culture, and growing your group's grit. However, it takes some tough intellectual thought for you and your team to develop a powerful, impactful purpose statement. Here are some corporate purpose statements to help you think about crafting your own organization's powerful purpose statement.

- IBM: Building a smarter planet.

- Southwest: To connect people to what's important in their lives through friendly, reliable, and low-cost air travel.
- Whole Foods: Our purpose is to nourish people and the planet.
- Netflix: Make great films with great people.
- Bayer Crop Science: Science for a better life.

ORGANIZATIONAL PURPOSE EXERCISE

It takes a 360-degree approach with your entire team to figure out your organization's purpose. The purpose is nebulous, but you can start to frame it by asking questions around the periphery. It's not easy—this is tough, demanding, intellectual work. Surveying other organizations, as well as having talks with your leadership team, your rank-and-file members, and your marketing team, are critical to uncovering your group's purpose.

Other Organizations

A good start place is to take a look at other organizations in your market. Trends in other organizations are superb indicators of what is driving action and connection in similar audiences. Looking at comparable organizations can help identify gaps and uncover the emotional appeals they are using. Three questions to ask your team as you examine the competition:

- What seems to be the purpose of others in this space?
- What are these organizations missing? What are their gaps?
- What trends are emerging, and what seems to be driving them?

Leadership

Talking to your leadership team can also provide insight into your organization's purpose. They may have different perspectives and different goals than you, but these can influence your organization's why. Use these five questions with your leadership team to get conversation flowing:

- What do you believe our brand does that no one else can?
- What makes us different?
- How does our company or our product change the lives of our customers and all who encounter it?
- What are we trying to change in the marketplace and our world with the work we do?
- Why did you start working in this company? Why did you choose this industry?

The Rank and File

During a visit to the NASA Space Center in 1962, President John F. Kennedy noticed a janitor carrying a broom. He interrupted his tour, walked over to the man, and said, "Hi, I'm Jack Kennedy. What are you doing?"

"Well, Mr. President," the janitor responded, "I'm helping put a man on the moon."

NASA's purpose resonated through the 400,000 people working on the Apollo program. Your purpose must resonate at every level of your organization—from the CEO to the janitor. Talk to as many people as possible to get an idea what marketing, accounting, sales, manufacturing, and yes, even the custodial team, thinks your purpose is. Use these questions to get the ideas flowing.

- Why did you choose our organization over others?

- What purpose do you feel you're fulfilling every day?
- What inspires what you do?
- What about our organization motivates you?

Marketing

Your purpose can be hidden in the way you're talking about your brand. The "bumper sticker slogans" that marketing uses are enlightening. In the 1960s, Avis was a smaller car rental company than the giant Hertz. In 1962, they embraced their smaller size and started running ads that said, "When you're only #2, you try harder." This resonated so deeply that Avis used this advertising campaign for fifty years. Take some time with the marketing team to read your materials and determine the following.

- What common themes appear in the way we talk about ourselves?
- What is the emotional driver behind those themes?
- How is the language we're using different than the language of our competitors?
- What solutions are we offering to solve our customer's problems?

Once you have multiple perspectives on your organization, sift the wheat from the chaff and determine what commonalities exist. Maybe you have incredible work ethic across the organization. Maybe your product is slightly different than the competition. Maybe you take a more strategic approach. Take these ideas and weave them into a coherent purpose. For instance, an organization might combine the three previous ideas to create a corporate purpose of "Built for the Long Haul."

Then test your new or revised organizational purpose on the leadership team. See what works, what doesn't, and what gets the team excited. Then refine it. When you're finally satisfied with your purpose statement, publish it to the entire organization. Then communicate your purpose at every opportunity. Even when you're tired of hearing it, communicate it some more. Like NASA, everyone, including the custodial team, needs to understand and live up to the purpose.

OBSTACLE

For companies, one of the biggest challenges is balancing the need to make a profit and living up to your business's purpose. Sometimes the two align, as it did with Starbucks. However, most of the time, they don't. It requires tough decisions and strong leadership to balance the two. And it may require regularly revisiting the purpose statement to make sure it aligns with your organization and its evolving business environment.

CONCLUSION

Dominating the global coffee market needed an incredibly strong purpose statement. Starbucks rediscovered its purpose and used it to become ubiquitous in lives of millions in the United States and around the world. Your organization may not be focused on making the world's best cup of coffee, but putting the intellectual energy into developing or improving your purpose statement can increase your grit, build your culture, and deliver incredible results.

Chapter 13

DEVELOP YOUR LEADER'S INTENT

"Upon reading these accounts, one cannot fail to be impressed by the significant results achieved by the little groups of men ... who advanced in the opening minutes of Operation NEPTUNE (the invasion of Normandy) against whatever enemy confronted them without asking whether they were outnumbered, and then held their ground waiting for the larger forces to come up."

Anonymous Officer, "Comment on 82d Division Operations"

LITTLE GROUPS OF PARATROOPERS

Operation Overlord, or the D-Day invasion on June 6, 1944, was the largest seaborne invasion in history. The sheer magnitude of what was done in one twenty-four-hour period amazes me to this day—156,115 American, British, and Canadian soldiers landed by boat and airplane across a fifty-five-mile coastline defended by 50,000 German troops. There were crises across every drop zone and on each of the five beaches—Utah, Omaha, Gold, Juno, and Sword—but by the end of the day, the Allies had established a foothold in France and had begun the liberation of German-occupied Western Europe.

As a former paratrooper, I loved visiting the drop zones and reading about the objectives of the paratroopers on both flanks of the Normandy invasion. In the west, around 13,100 American paratroopers of the 82nd and 101st Airborne Divisions made night parachute drops behind Utah Beach, followed by 3,937 glider troops during the day. Behind Sword Beach (in the east), the British 6th Airborne Division inserted approximately 8,500 men by parachute and glider. The heroic achievements of both Dick Winters of Easy Company, 506th PIR, 101st Airborne Division (in the west) and Major John Howard of D Company, 2nd Battalion Oxfordshire and Buckinghamshire Light Infantry, 6th Airborne Division (in the east) were made famous in books by the historian Stephen Ambrose.

C-47, or DC-3, cargo planes could carry eighteen paratroopers. It took hundreds of planes to deliver a PIR. Even small errors between the pilots could result in paratroopers being scattered across the countryside during a nighttime combat, parachute assault. Whenever you drop thousands of paratroopers at night, there will be chaos, unexpected events, and adversity. Embracing the uncertainty, the 82nd and 101st Airborne Divisions planned for things not to go right during a parachute jump. To overcome the challenges of a night airborne assault, the leaders ensured that all paratroopers understood their commander's intent. That way, when little groups of paratroopers found each other in the middle of the night after missing the drop zone, a leader would take charge, start attacking anything that looked like it belonged to the German military, and do their best to accomplish the group's purpose and leader's intent. The legend of the little groups of paratroopers, aggressively operating under intent and demonstrating initiative, was solidified in the hedgerows of Normandy. A more unfamiliar paratrooper is Lieutenant Colonel Ben Vandervoort, the commander of the

2nd Battalion, 505th PIR, 82nd Airborne Division. With combat experience in Sicily, Vandervoort, then twenty-seven years old, led a unit of about 560 paratroopers in a mission to land at Drop Zone O and "capture and hold the town of Ste. Mere Eglise."

Lieutenant Colonel Ben Vandervoort's Commander's Intent in Normandy would have been simple. 2nd Battalion, 505th PIR's purpose was to protect the northwest flank of Utah Beach and the 4th Infantry Division landings. Its key tasks were to conduct a night parachute assault, assemble the battalion, seize the town of Ste. Mere Eglise, and defend the town from German counterattacks. On June 7, 1944, or D-Day+1, Ste. Mere Eglise and its road network needed to be in the battalion's possession.

Of course, even after months of planning and rehearsals, paratroopers were scattered across the French countryside in the early morning hours of June 6th. To make things more challenging, Vandervoort broke his foot during his landing. In spite of the adversities, he assembled a small group of men, moved overland, and, together with elements of the 3rd Battalion, 505th PIR, attacked and seized the small village of Ste. Mere Eglise and its crossroads. For the next several days, Vandervoort and his men defended north of the town against determined German attacks. For his actions in Normandy, Vandervoort received a Distinguished Service Cross (the nation's second highest award for valor). As one combat veteran and friend described him, he was "calm ... clear and decisive in combat and always led from the front in the standard 82nd fashion." John Wayne portrayed him in the 1962 movie *The Longest Day.*

Commander's intent empowers subordinates' improvisation and adaptation during complex operations under evolving conditions. Thanks to Lieutenant Colonel Vandervoort's paratroopers understanding his intent, when the sun came up on the morning of June 6th, Ste. Mere Eglise was under the control of the 2nd Battalion, 505th PIR. Little groups of paratroopers displayed disciplined initiative and decentralized execution in the chaos of combat on D-Day.

COMMANDER'S INTENT

The 2nd Battalion, 505th Parachute Infantry Regiment on June 6, 1944 used organizational grit to persevere and overcome obstacles. A critical part of organizational grit is providing the group a purpose, a plan, and a scoreboard. One way to do this is to borrow the military's concept of commander's intent which combines all three into one elegant package.

Current army doctrine defines the commander's intent as, "a clear, concise statement of what the force must do and the conditions the force must establish with respect to the enemy, terrain, and civil considerations that represent the desired end state. The commander's intent succinctly describes what constitutes success for the operation. It includes the operation's purpose and the conditions that define the end state. It links the mission, concept of operations, and tasks to subordinate units." Commanders strive to ensure that not just their direct reports, but their direct-direct reports understand the commander's intent. During my time in the army, I was expected to understand my boss's intent and my boss's boss's intent and make sure that my direct- and direct-direct reports understood my intent. Understanding the purpose, or the "why," two levels up and down provides a powerful advantage.

In Afghanistan, the battalion I commanded used commander's intent to empower, adapt, and improvise as we fought in Paktika Province. Our purpose was to increase the safety and security in that region. Our key task was to conduct counterinsurgency operations in conjunction with our Afghan-government partners. Our end state specified that by December 31, 2010 the battalion and our Afghan partners would decrease violence in the province by 10 percent (the decrease in violence would be seen as the population siding with the government against the Taliban).

This commander's intent empowered my direct reports to operate without constantly calling me and asking for permission as the situation evolved. When a group of Taliban insurgents presented themselves, my direct reports could attack them without hesitation because it was contributing to the increased safety and security of the province. Additionally, if a mission was overcome by unexpected events, my direct reports were free to improvise as long as their actions aligned with the intent. Understanding the commander's intent is an exceptionally powerful tool in an ambiguous environment.

LEADER'S INTENT

The leader's intent, or intent, works well for corporate, nonprofit, and sports teams too. Like the commander's intent, the leader's intent has three parts: the purpose, or a "why"; key tasks, or the "what" or the "how"; and a defined end state, or what success looks like. A leader's intent describes how the CEO or leader envisions the environment at a point in time in the future. It shows what represents success. A leader's intent fully recognizes how chaos, a lack of complete information, and changes in what the competition is doing may make a plan either completely or partially obsolete as it is being executed. Leader's intent empowers subordinates and guides their initiative and improvisation as they adapt the plan to the ever-changing environment. Like the military, understanding the leader's intent at least two levels up and two levels down increases alignment.

If you are the leader, make sure you have a deep understanding of the three aspects of the leader's intent:

1. The purpose, or the "why" (*think about a slightly broader purpose than in a mission statement. It needs to enable*

people to make decisions in your absence. Chapter 13 has a purpose exercise).

2. Key Tasks that must be accomplished (*maybe one for each department, division, or section*). There are two ways to think about key tasks. First, each of your silos, or independent business units, may need a key task, or you may need to break down the end state into a series of steps that need to be accomplished during a specific time period. Make sure that each task is specific, measurable, attainable, relevant, and time bound.
3. The end state, or what success looks like (*I find it helpful for the end state to be measurable and be tied to a date in the future*). End state describes how the world will look at a certain date in the future. It takes tough intellectual work to develop an end state that you, your direct reports, and their direct reports can envision and helps move the organization in a positive direction. Finding the right metric to use may require an iterative process. For military units, it is helpful to conceptualize an end state that looks at friendly forces, enemy forces, and the environment. Sports teams may find it useful to conceptualize the future from the perspective of your team, the competition, and the fans. Businesses may find it helpful to conceptualize the future from the perspective of your business, the competition, and the clients or users. Finally, nonprofits may find it useful to think about the future from the perspective of your group, what you are supporting, and the donors.

LEADER'S INTENT EXAMPLES

Here are three examples of leader's intent that demonstrate its utility in different situations.

For corporate groups, here is a small manufacturing company's leader's intent from early 2020:

- Purpose: ACME Manufacturing will keep the team safe and employed.
- Key Tasks:
    - Aggressively market our products.
    - Sales team must get orders, especially in the second quarter.
    - Cost containment—use our money frugally.
- End State: By December 30, 2020 ensure ACME Manufacturing has met 75 percent of 2019 sales and production.

By using the leader's intent and communicating it to the team ACME Manufacturing was able to make 103 percent of its 2019 sales, as well as improve their efficiency during the pandemic.

Another example is Apple Computers in late 2006. They had just released the MacBook Pro laptops, transitioned to Intel processor chips, and the iPod and iTunes were doing well. The company needed to keep innovating, so hypothetically they might have used a leader's intent that looked something like this:

- Purpose: Challenge the status quo and increase shareholder value.
- Key Tasks:
    - Build user friendly, beautifully designed, easy-to-use devices.
    - Expand services platforms.
- End State: Annual revenue up 17 percent by December 31, 2007.

Thorough understanding of their purpose enabled Apple to release the iPhone in 2007, disrupt the status quo, and generate enormous profits.

Finally, think of Love's Travel Stops in 2020.

- Purpose: Grow the company profitably and innovatively while maintaining the brand's reputation for highway hospitality.
- Key Tasks (for each of its silos):
    - Love's Travel Stops—Be the cleanest and friendliest spot on the highway for fuel, food, and snacks; invest in our people, and grow by 8 percent.
    - Gemini—Continue to safely transport petroleum products across the nation.
    - Musket—Purchase energy resources innovatively and profitably.
    - Trillium—Develop into a market leader for innovative energy solutions.
- End State: By December 31, 2020 open forty new stores, add 3,000 parking spots, create 2,500 new jobs.

Communicating their leader's intent to multiple levels of the organization enabled Love's to meet all their goals in spite of the pandemic.

The three examples of leaders' intent show the language and impact leveraging this powerful tool can provide to you and your team. Developing a great leader's intent is an iterative process and one that requires input from and collaboration with your team.

DEVELOPING YOUR LEADER'S INTENT

Drafting a leader's intent in a vacuum rarely works. Instead, it must be a team effort. Once you have your organization's purpose sorted out (see Chapter 12), it is important to bring the group together and discuss the key tasks that must be accomplished and what the collective vision for the future is. Getting the group's buy-in makes it much easier to get the group to strive toward accomplishing the leader's intent. I find that this exercise works best in a room with a large wall and large pieces of paper for groups or individual leaders to write on.

Your Leader's Intent

Leader's Intent:

- Purpose (*The why*):
- Key Tasks (*The what. One for each part of your group?*):
- End State (*What does success look like in the future?*): By December 31, 2021...

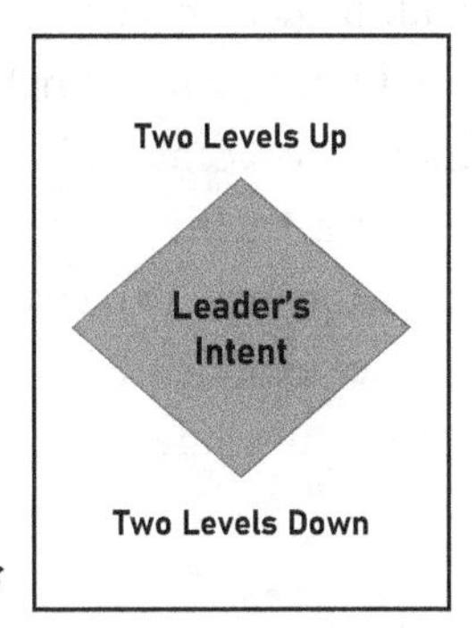

Leader's Intent

To begin this exercise, have each member of the team read this chapter. Then bring the team into a large room and spend some time talking about your understanding of the concept of leader's intent. Take large pieces of paper (or white boards) and place them around the room along with markers. Divide the leadership team into small groups and give them twenty minutes to come up with a leader's intent for the entire team (your leader's intent). Have each group brief you and the rest of the group on their version of the leader's intent. Select one group's leader's intent or build a hybrid to use as the overall group's leader's intent.

Once you have settled on the overall leader's intent, place it on the wall where everyone can see it. Then, send each leader back out to a fresh piece of paper for another twenty minutes to create the leader's intent for their portion of the organization (one-level down). Have each leader brief one of their peers on their leader's intent, get feedback, and then swap. Once they refine them, have each direct report talk you through their leader's intent. In a couple of hours, you can have aligned leader's intents for the overall organization and the next level down.

Once you have finalized the leader's intent, communicate, communicate, communicate it to the organization. Having a leader's intent is the first step. Everyone knowing the leader's intent one level and even two levels down are the next step and increases the impact exponentially. "Short and memorable" is important if you want your leader's intent to cascade throughout the organization.

OBSTACLE

One challenge that leaders encounter is that their boss often doesn't provide a leader's intent. It even happens in the army where it is part of the processes and culture. For example, my boss didn't publish his intent until we had been on the ground in Afghanistan for two months. I published mine five months earlier because I wanted my battalion to have my intent as we planned, deployed, and executed our first engagements on the ground. When my boss finally published his, I modified mine to align and nest with his. No matter what the environment or circumstance, don't wait for your boss to publish their intent. Do the right thing, publish your intent, and empower your team to act with disciplined initiative in an evolving environment.

CONCLUSION

Your team is not parachuting into the hedgerows of Normandy. Yet providing a leader's intent to sports teams, nonprofits, and corporate groups will enhance your organization's sense of empowerment, initiative, and adaptation as the environment changes and evolves. Go on the offensive and enhance your organization's grit by providing them a leader's intent that combines a purpose, a roadmap, and a goal.

Chapter 14

BASIC PLANNING

"In preparing for battle I have always found that plans are useless, but planning is indispensable."

General Dwight D. Eisenhower

GENERAL DWIGHT "IKE" EISENHOWER WAS a military planner. After the attack on Peral Harbor in December 1941, he served as the head of the army's War Plans division and built the war plans to defeat Germany and Japan. He was so talented as a planner that he was selected to lead Operation Torch, the Allied invasion of North Africa, and, eventually, Operation Overlord, the invasion of France. Despite the months of planning for establishing the beachhead in Normandy, Ike knew the invasion would not go as planned. In his letter to the troops prior to the operation, he told them, "Your task will not be an easy one. Your enemy is well trained, well equipped and battle-hardened. He will fight savagely ... I have full confidence in your courage, devotion to duty and skill in battle. We will accept nothing less than full victory!" Eisenhower, of course, went on to lead the Allies' victory in Europe, as well as serve two terms as president of the United States. Not bad for a military planner.

Planning in the military, business, nonprofits, and other environments has gotten a bad reputation. Unforeseen events derail the most carefully laid plans. Organizations struggle to accomplish the tasks laid out in the plans. Annual planning cycles fail to anticipate trends. Planners rarely change the plan significantly year-in and year-out. Plans only produce budgets and financial forecasts. A recent survey of executives confirmed the dissatisfaction in planning: only 45 percent were satisfied with their planning process and only 23 percent thought key decisions were made during it.

Yet for the vast number of organizations, the annual planning process plays an essential role. In addition to building some elements of a company's strategy, the process results in a budget, allocates resources for the coming twelve-to-eighteen months, sets financial and operating goals, and aligns leadership on the organization's strategic priorities. Although many decisions are made outside the planning process, having the planning framework enables companies, especially when using the leader's intent, to deviate from the plan, seize opportunities, and avoid miscalculations. Planning, at its essence, is setting priorities, deciding what not to do (one of the hardest parts), and building contingencies for a year that looks different than the previous year. Having a planning process and a format to convey the plan are the first steps in planning, developing a roadmap for your team, and increasing your organization's grit.

PLANNING PROCESS

If you are a leader in a small or medium sized organization, a sports team, or a nonprofit, you may not have a standardized planning process yet. Establishing and implementing an effective and repeatable planning process is vital to the success of any team because it enables everyone in the enterprise to think through the problem and apply the assets of the organization toward solving the problem while using the same formats and terminology. The military has this with the Troop Leading Procedures (TLPs) for small units and the Military Decision-Making Process (MDMP) for large units.

For the past seven decades, the US Army's Ranger School taught and still continues to teach the TLP and the Operations Order (OPORD) format as a way to convey plans to a small group. The process and the OPORD format were something continuously drilled into my brain as I struggled through the mountains of North Georgia and the swamps of Florida in 1994; but the dozens of repetitions paid off—I became thoroughly indoctrinated in the process and format. Throughout my career, I used the planning process and OPORD format to provide a plan to my platoon during the aborted airborne invasion of Haiti in 1994, a German tank unit in Bosnia in 2002, repeatedly to a battalion in combat in eastern Baghdad in 2005, repeatedly to a brigade in counterinsurgency operations in the suburbs of Baghdad in 2007 and 2008, and regularly to my battalion in Afghanistan in 2010 and 2011.

For a variety of reasons, the military planning process is an imperfect fit for other environments. However, modifying the military's planning process to fit your business, nonprofit, or team can be a great start point for establishing a standardized way to think through problems both long- and short-term. As General George S. Patton once said, "A good plan, violently executed now, is better than a perfect plan next week."

PLANNING CHECKLIST

A checklist for an organizational planning process to develop a good plan, right now, might look like this:

- ☐ [Leader and the Team] Analyze the problem, the environment, and the mission or the task.
  - Facts and Assumptions. (*Basic facts and assumptions about the organization and environment.)*
  - Market. *(What's your market outlook? What assumptions are you building the plan upon?)*
  - Customer. *(What's your customer doing?)*
  - Competition. (*Who's your competition? What are they doing?)*
  - Regulatory. (*What rules did we follow last year? What rules are new for this year?*)
  - Corporate *(or the board of directors). (What are they doing? What's their mission?)*
  - Resources. *(What is your budget? How many people do you have available?)*
  - Historic. *(What did you do last year? What worked? What didn't work?)*
- ☐ [Leader and the Team] Goal Setting: After analysis, think through the group's goals.
  - *Are your goals SMART? (A SMART goal means that the goal is specific, measurable, attainable, relevant, and time bound. See Chapter 3 for more ideas on SMART goals.)*
    - Specific: What will be accomplished? What actions will you take?
    - Measurable: What data will measure the goal? (How much? How well?)

        - Achievable: Is the goal doable? Do you have the necessary skills and resources?
        - Relevant: How does the goal align with our organization's purpose? Does it align with our organization's vision? Why are the results important?
        - Time bound: What is the time frame for accomplishing the goal?
    - What is your stretch goal or a goal that exceeds expectations?
    - What will the organization not do this year to enable the accomplishment of more important goals?
    - If you have challenges setting goals in your organization, limit yourself to one piece of paper or one index card for your goals.
- ☐ [Leader and the Team] Develop a course of action (broad guidelines) to solve the problem, accomplish the mission, complete the task, or drive your organization during the year.
    - Outline key things to accomplish.
    - Outline key limitations.
    - Outline things to avoid.
- ☐ [Leader] Develop your Mission and Leader's Intent (See Chapter 13).
    - Mission. (*The Who, What, When, Where, and How that will guide you.*)
    - Purpose. *(A broader why then the one used in the mission statement. Enables decisions in your absence.)*
    - Key Tasks. *(The How.)*
    - End State. *(What does success look like at a certain date in the future?)*
- ☐ [Team] Empower your team to develop the plan by providing planning guidance. (*What key elements do you want*

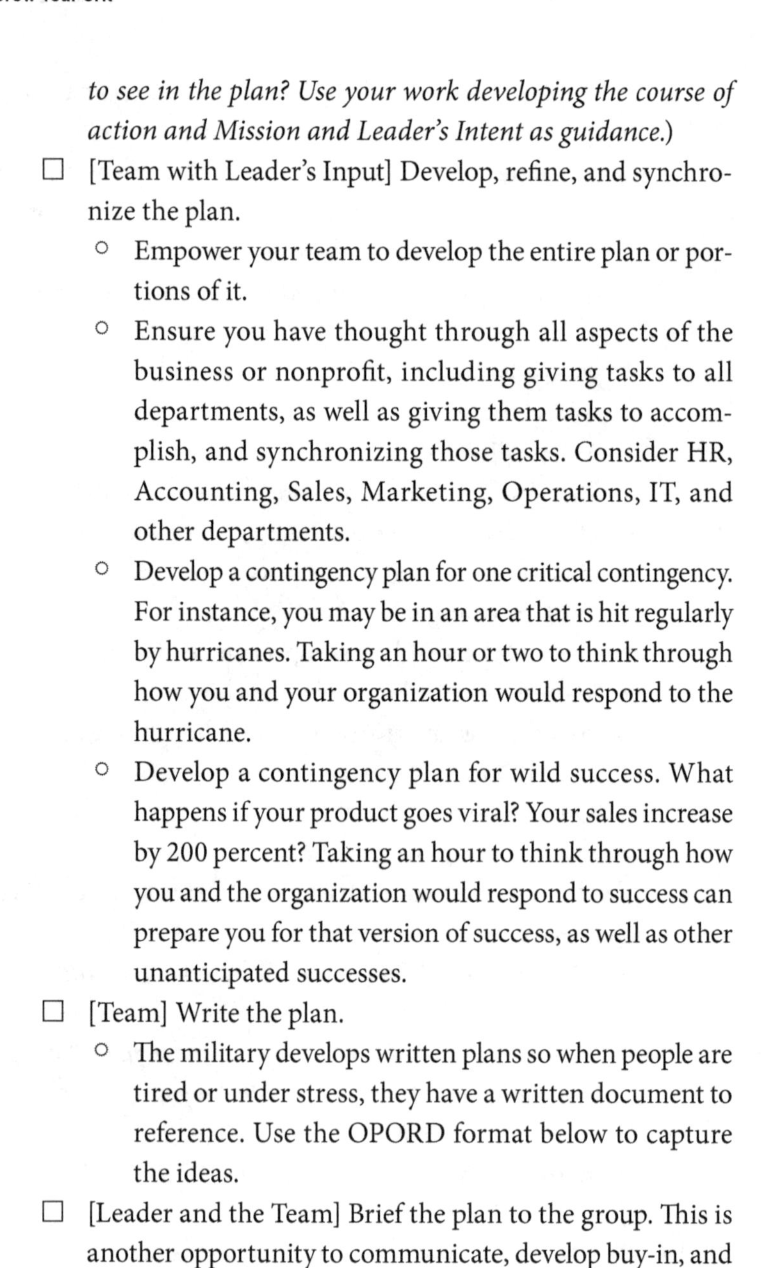

to see in the plan? Use your work developing the course of action and Mission and Leader's Intent as guidance.)

☐ [Team with Leader's Input] Develop, refine, and synchronize the plan.

- ○ Empower your team to develop the entire plan or portions of it.
- ○ Ensure you have thought through all aspects of the business or nonprofit, including giving tasks to all departments, as well as giving them tasks to accomplish, and synchronizing those tasks. Consider HR, Accounting, Sales, Marketing, Operations, IT, and other departments.
- ○ Develop a contingency plan for one critical contingency. For instance, you may be in an area that is hit regularly by hurricanes. Taking an hour or two to think through how you and your organization would respond to the hurricane.
- ○ Develop a contingency plan for wild success. What happens if your product goes viral? Your sales increase by 200 percent? Taking an hour to think through how you and the organization would respond to success can prepare you for that version of success, as well as other unanticipated successes.

☐ [Team] Write the plan.

- ○ The military develops written plans so when people are tired or under stress, they have a written document to reference. Use the OPORD format below to capture the ideas.

☐ [Leader and the Team] Brief the plan to the group. This is another opportunity to communicate, develop buy-in, and ensure alignment.

- ○ [Leader] Emphasize your Mission and Leader's Intent.

  - [Team] Ensure that the key leaders say back to you in their own words the key portion of the plan to ensure that everyone understands.
- ☐ [Leader] Supervise preparation for, rehearsals of, and execution of the plan.
- ☐ [Leader and the Team] Conduct an After Action Review of the planning and execution. Capture lessons learned and implement them in the organization's next planning process.

COMMUNICATING THE PLAN—THE OPERATIONS ORDER

The Operations Order (OPORD) is a standard format for conveying information for a military plan. It consists of five paragraphs—Situation, Mission, Execution, Service and Support (or Admin and Logistics by the US Marine Corps), and Command and Control. Most people don't know that the Army's standard format for an Operations Order was developed by Frederick Garman in 1957 when he was assigned to Fort Benning's Ranger Department (the predecessor of today's US Army Ranger School.) The Army quickly adopted it, and it has been used in every conflict since the Vietnam War. Talk about an idea going viral!

In Afghanistan, the unit I was part of used the OPORD to convey yearlong campaign plans, as well as short-duration missions. Using the same format for a plan enabled everyone to know where to listen for the information they needed if they were receiving it orally, or where to look for the information if they had a written copy. More importantly, using the OPORD format forced us to think through all the elements of the plan.

This OPORD format nests well with the planning process discussed earlier. Every department in a business can use both of them to support their future planning. Whether you are the leader of a human resources department, the sales team, marketing, or production, using a similar format can ensure that your plans are aligned, synchronized, and nested with the rest of your teams.

Utilizing a corporate OPORD format will help you build a better plan for your team. Keeping the OPORD to one or two pages provides your corporate team enough of a framework, raises the odds that the team actually reads the document, and enables your people to retain their agility and initiative while acting within the leader's intent. I modified the military format to better fit a corporate environment. For those of you familiar with the military OPORD, I combined Paragraph 4, Logistics, and Paragraph 5, Command and Control, into one Paragraph 4, titled Admin, Logistics, and Communications. Feel free to optimize this format so it fits your unique situation.

CORPORATE OPERATIONS ORDER FORMAT

1. Situation:
    - Market. *(What's your market outlook? What assumptions are you building the plan upon?)*
    - Customer. *(What's your customer doing?)*
    - Competition. *(Who's your competition? What are they doing?)*
    - Higher Levels in the Company. *(What are they doing? What's their mission?)*
2. Mission: *(Who, What, When, Where, and Why.)*
3. Execution:
    - Leader's Intent (See Chapter 13)
        - Purpose. *(A broader Why then the one used in the mission statement. Enables initiative and decisions in your absence.)*
        - Key Tasks. *(The How.)*

    - End State. *(What does success look like on December 31?)*
- Major Events by Month (*Consider for the executive group, HR, IT, marketing, sales, and operations*).
    - January
    - February
    - March
    - April
    - May
    - June
    - July
    - August
    - September
    - October
    - November
    - December
        - Conduct After Action Review (See Chapter 15).
        - Build annual plan for next year.
- Key Tasks for different portions of the business to accomplish:
    - Operations.
    - Marketing.
    - Sales.
    - HR.
    - IT.
    - Accounting and Finance.

4. Admin, Logistics, and Communications:
    - Administrative Issues/Tasks.
    - Logistics to support the plan.
    - Communications to the:
        - Shareholders/board.
        - Market.
        - Company.

This format is used today by leaders in real estate, healthcare, agribusiness, and the petroleum industry.

OBSTACLE

One of the biggest obstacles with plans are that most are too complex. Their complexity leads to them being overcome by events and not being very useful as the team executes the plan in a steadily evolving environment. When that happens, your team doesn't put a lot of effort into planning because they don't see a return on the investment. Keep your plans simple so they retain flexibility as the environment changes. Remember, if Ike's plan for the invasion of Europe was only five pages in length, yours can be that short or shorter for whatever you are trying to accomplish.

CONCLUSION

Your organization is most likely not planning anything on the scale of the invasion of Europe in 1944, but utilizing a planning process can give your organization the framework to deal with chaos, seize opportunities, and improvise. In addition, like General Eisenhower commented, the work done thinking through contingencies for both a crisis and a success is "indispensable." Use a standard planning process and the OPORD format to get your team to better understand the goals and the roadmap you will follow, as well as enhance its organizational grit.

Chapter 15

THE CULTURE OF GRIT

"I believe that this nation should commit itself to achieving the goal, before this decade is out, of landing a man on the moon and returning him safely to the Earth."

John F. Kennedy, May 25, 1961

"We choose to go to the Moon. We choose to go to the Moon ... We choose to go to the Moon in this decade and do the other things, not because they are easy, but because they are hard; because that goal will serve to organize and measure the best of our energies and skills, because that challenge is one that we are willing to accept, one we are unwilling to postpone, and one we intend to win ..."

John F. Kennedy, September 12, 1962

NASA'S GOAL WAS TO LAND humans on the moon during the Apollo program, which lasted from 1961 to 1972. At a cost of $25.4 billion ($156 billion in today's dollars), the program landed six missions and twelve astronauts on the lunar surface and returned them safely to the Earth. The program helped us gain a better understanding of the moon, the challenges of spaceflight, and large project management concepts. It also led to the creation of 1,800 spinoff products including semiconductors and integrated circuits. In the end, the Apollo program, in both size (over 400,000 people) and cost, rivaled the building of the Panama Canal or the Manhattan Project's efforts to construct the first atomic bomb.

Critical to aligning the 400,000 people both in NASA and its contractors was the purpose articulated by President John F. Kennedy in 1961 and reinforced in 1962. Once aligned with the purpose, NASA's culture helped keep the program focused, gritty, and able to overcome obstacles. NASA's organizational culture revolved around maintaining and improving its in-house, world-class, technical capabilities; utilizing systems management techniques to control schedules, track costs, and ensure the highest levels of performance; and leveraging incredibly tight relationships with hundreds of contractors. NASA's in-house culture drew upon tough accountability for successes and failures, an incredibly high standard for competence, and perseverance to overcome obstacles and keep everyone aligned. Over its eleven years, NASA's organizational culture ensured the Apollo program met its purpose of "landing a man on the moon and returning him safely to the Earth."

Culture is defined as the beliefs, values, and behaviors that determine how an organization's people interact and behave both inside and outside the organization. It's not something an organization says or tries to be. It is something an organization does. Culture influences organizational performance, innovation, agility, engagement, and competitiveness. Research shows that a toxic culture decreases productivity by 40 percent, while an effective culture increases productivity by 20 percent. It's clear that having a great culture gives you and your team a competitive advantage.

In my opinion, a great organizational culture is built upon three principles: purpose, values, and a safe, connected, and engaged environment. It's worth taking a deeper look at the meaning of each of these terms.

- Purpose: the *why* for your company or your organization.
- Values: the principles or standards of behavior that drive the organization.
- Safe, connected, and engaged environment: an environment where the group is engaged, each individual talks and listens, members talk directly to each other, and providing feedback is safe.

Whether you are NASA, a military organization, a nonprofit, a corporate group, or a sports team, revisiting or developing your purpose, values, and environment is critical to building the group's culture and grit.

ORGANIZATIONAL VALUES

Drafting organizational values in a vacuum rarely works. Instead, it must be a team effort. Once you have determined your organization's purpose, it is important to bring the group together and discuss the values that you practice, the values you want to eliminate, and the values you aspire to have. Getting the group's buy-in makes it much easier to get the group to live the values.

Six steps are helpful in developing or refining your values. I find that this exercise works best in a room with a large wall and dozens of Post-it Notes for every participant.

First, what is your organization's purpose? If you don't have one, use the exercise in Chapter 12 to create one. If you have one, write it down and put it up on the wall with Post-it Notes. Ensure the group still finds the purpose relevant.

Second, set a stopwatch for ten minutes and have everyone take Post-it Notes and answer three questions:

- What values have contributed to our success to date (or in the last twelve months)?
- What values do the people in this group share in common?
- What values should govern how we interact with each other and our customers in the next twelve months?

Typical values are integrity, creativity, customer service, boldness, trust, fun, passion, quality, teamwork, growth, innovation, responsibility, and simplicity. Gritty values are work ethic, accountability, and constant improvement. Have everyone write their answers on Post-it Notes and put them on the wall.

Third, designate one person to organize all the core values into groups. For instance, if three people have written integrity (or something similar), they should be grouped together.

Once all the values are organized into groups, it is time to whittle the list down to the top five core values. Why five? I find that it is the most that members of the group can remember. You may need to vote to trim the number of values down to five.

Fifth, discuss implementing the values into the organization by asking this series of questions to the group about each of the five core values:

- What does this value mean to us?
- What does this value look like in practice?
- How might this value be misinterpreted?
- How will we evaluate how well people follow this value?
- How will this value change our organization's relationships and interactions?

Now, take a break—you deserve it after all the hard work. A week later, circulate a draft of your purpose and your five core values along with the answers to the five questions to the team. Solicit feedback. Then, revise, revise, revise your values.

The more thoughtful and intentional the process is, the better. After the team has had some time to digest the established purpose and values, bring the group back together to talk through them one last time. If the group is aligned and has buy-in, publish the values. You, as the leader, then need to communicate the values to the leaders and the team at every opportunity.

HISTORY AND CULTURE

Stories are powerful. An organization's history is a formidable story too. Once you have determined your purpose and values, you can gain an advantage in growing your culture by looking back at, and drawing from, your organization's history. In *The Culture Code*, Dan Coyle argues that organizations with great cultures celebrate their history and use it as a foundation for where they have been, what they stand for, and where they are going. I agree.

The Army's personnel system makes everyone's assignment to a unit temporary. Soldiers typically serve in one unit for two to three years and then move on to another unit. To help build the culture of the organization, the unit relies on its history. Every army unit you visit—companies, battalions, brigades, and divisions—will have a portion of their offices dedicated to the history of that outfit. Not only is the history on display, but the soldiers and leaders of the unit are required to know its history, such as what battles it fought in, the heroic actions of its soldiers, and what awards the unit received.

For instance, the battalion I led—3rd Battalion, 187th Infantry Regiment, known as the Iron Rakkasans—fought during World War II, Korea, Vietnam, Desert Storm, Iraq, and Afghanistan.

Over those campaigns, the battalion conducted three airborne assaults, fought the battle of Hamburger Hill in Vietnam, cleared Saddam International Airport in Baghdad in 2003, and saw two Iron Rakkasans earn the Medal of Honor. The walls of the battalion headquarters building, the conference rooms, and the company offices are covered with historic images and tokens from battles fought around the world over the last nine decades.

Yet the history on the walls wasn't just there for aesthetics. It was a way for the organization to tell its own story—that tough training enabled the Iron Rakkasans to overcome adversity and accomplish the mission no matter what era. It also reminded the constant influx of new members of what the team that came before them represented. Finally, it helped to create the unit's direction forward as it trained to meet its next "rendezvous with destiny."

I recently did some work with Love's Travel Stops. Their walls are covered with pictures from their history: the first store, the 200th store, its acquisition of other companies, and its charity work. Each picture reinforced to the team their humble beginnings, their corporate culture centered on family values, and their strong desire for dramatic growth over the next five years.

One aspect that companies could borrow from the military and Love's is using their corporate history as a way to enhance their culture. What historic events are important in your company and support your purpose and values? Do your entrance, hallways, and conference rooms celebrate this history? What recent events should be added to the history? How are you using the history and its stories to reinforce your purpose and values?

Recognizing and getting the history on the walls is the easy step. Take the next step and figure out how to use it to complement your organization's purpose, values, and culture.

THE AFTER ACTION REVIEW

Organizations have used the debrief, the postmortem, and the After Action Review as ways to learn and grow from experiences both good and bad. These techniques are the strongest means of creating a safe, engaged environment where real bonds and trust grow between the members. Using both positive and negative events to develop your organization into a learning organization is critical in building culture and grit.

During World War II, the US Army Air Force (USAAF) pursued daylight bombing of Germany's industries to attrit military production. In eighteen months, the 8th Air Force grew from seven people to 185,000 people and 4,000 planes. Flying B-17 Flying Fortresses from bases in England, the wings and squadrons struggled to put bombs on their targets while suffering almost 27,000 fatalities. For example, on the second Schweinfurt Raid in October 1943, 198 of 291 B-17s were damaged or destroyed. To make matters worse, the bombs failed to destroy their target, ball bearing factories. In early 1944, Major General Jimmy Doolittle took over and turned the unit's performance around. The 8th Air Force played a critical role in the bombing of Berlin, damaging railyards before D-Day, destroying the German oil industry, and defeating the Luftwaffe.

One of the key ways the 8th Air Force improved its performance was through the use of an interrogation or debrief, an event that happened after every mission in World War II. When the B-17 Flying Fortresses landed, aircrews were taken to a building, given food and coffee, and then seated at a table with a debriefing officer. The debriefing officer, using a preprinted Interrogation Form, thoroughly questioned the crew about what happened during the mission, what went right, and what needed to be done differently in the future. Everyone got to talk and contribute. The debriefs were compiled, and the lessons learned were used to improve the effectiveness of the unit during the next bombing raid. Over time, the interrogations improved the 8th Air Force's performance and hastened the end of the war.

Flash forward to today, and US Army uses a similar tool called the After Action Review, or AAR, as a way to provide structured performance feedback for units after training events and combat operations. Corporate groups have adopted it as well. I'm convinced it is a great tool for your organization to use to build a safe, engaged environment, as well as enhance your culture and grit.

When should you do an AAR as an organization? A few of many examples are after every big event, a new product roll-out, a response to a pandemic, or poor crisis communications. The AAR should happen as close to the event as possible, so the experience is still fresh in everyone's mind. Your organization needs five things before trying to do an AAR:

- One or two hours when the group can gather.
- A facilitator *(not the leader, but typically a senior person in the organization).*
- Data and facts about how the organization performed during the event.
- Motivated participants.
- A notetaker.

The facilitator will gather the group in a room, reduce external distractions, and use four questions to guide the AAR's conversation:

- What was the plan? *(Typically, this question is posed to the leader, who takes the team through the plan. This usually takes five to ten minutes to talk through.)*
- What happened? *(The facilitator tries to get as many participants as possible to talk about what happened at their level. What did they see or do? What didn't they do? Breaking*

the events down by day or week is helpful to energize the discussion. This usually takes fifteen to twenty minutes to talk through. Once the entire event is discussed, move to the next two questions.)

- What is one thing you should sustain, in my role or at my level, the next time the event or situation occurs? (*Asked of every participant. These two questions should take thirty to sixty minutes to talk through. This question and the next one are the real secret to the power of the AAR.*)
- What is one thing you should improve, in my role or at my level, the next time the event or situation occurs? *(Asked of every participant.)*

After the AAR is complete, the notetaker and facilitator should publish the notes. Future plans, processes, and procedures should be updated based on the results of the AAR.

Whether you call it an interrogation like the bomber pilots of World War II, or an After Action Review like the modern US Army, the goal is the same: get the team to learn together what happened, give everyone a chance to contribute, identify what went right and commit to repeating it, and have accountability for what needs to be done better the next time. Your organization's performance and culture will benefit from your implementation of the AAR as part of your normal operations.

ORGANIZATIONAL CULTURE EXAMPLES

Culture is what an organization does, not what it says it does. It exists in every organization, such as military units, corporations, and sports teams. Examining examples of each type of group, both good and bad, can provide insight into how to build and grow your organizational culture.

The US Army is a global organization of 450,000 people. It has an annual budget of $178 billion. Its culture could be described as:

- Purpose: Be prepared to and, if called upon, fight and win our nation's wars.
- Values: The US Army's stated values are Loyalty, Duty, Respect, Selfless Service, Honor, Integrity, and Personal Courage. In addition, its unofficial values/behavior include physical fitness in the morning, extensive use of PowerPoint, hurry up and wait, and timeliness. One method that groups use to reinforce these values is by using the history of the organization to tell stories that reinforce the desired values.
- Safe, connected, and engaged environment: The army's safe, connected feedback method that encourages group learning is the After Action Review.

A company that is well known for its superb corporate culture is Pixar. Pixar is a computer animation studio and subsidiary of the Walt Disney Corporation that has produced twenty-two outstanding animated films over its thirty-four years of existence, including *Toy Story*, *Brave*, *The Incredibles*, and *Coco*. The films have earned approximately $14 billion at the box office. Pixar is known for cultivating a creative culture.

Pixar's culture could be described as:

- Purpose: Make great films with great people.
- Values:
    - Great people are a priority.
    - Collaboration among the team.
    - Take risks.
    - Have fun.

- Safe, connected, and engaged environment: Pixar utilizes open office spaces, constructive feedback mechanisms to develop their films, postmortems to discuss their failures, and open communication throughout the entire organization to encourage a creative, collaborative environment.

While it's easy to praise companies that have great corporate culture, it's important to also look at companies that are struggling. Enron was an energy, services, and commodities company whose stock value made it the seventh-largest company in America at one time. However, the company moved liabilities off the balance sheet and hid the fact that it was booking revenues for multiple years ahead. These actions hugely inflated profits and Enron's share price. Once its deception was revealed, Enron filed for bankruptcy in 2001, causing the disbandment of the Arthur Anderson accounting firm as well. Many of Enron's senior leaders were prosecuted for their roles in the deception. If you want to learn more, *Enron: The Smartest Guys in the Room* is a fantastic documentary about the company's rise and fall. Enron's actions demonstrated that it prioritized greed and pushing the boundaries as far as possible over its stated values of respect and integrity. The values can't be just words—they have to be what the company does every day.

Looking at Enron's cultural shortcomings provides another perspective on culture:

- Purpose: To become the world's leading energy company, creating innovative and efficient energy solutions for growing economies and create a better environment worldwide.
- Values: Enron's stated values in its 2000 Annual Report were:
    - Communication: We have an obligation to communicate.
    - Respect: We treat others as we would like to be treated.

  - Integrity: We work with customers and prospects openly, honestly, and sincerely.
  - Excellence: We are satisfied with nothing less than the very best in everything we do.
- Safe, connected, and engaged environment: Enron's policy of eliminating the bottom 20 percent of the employees every year created a very competitive environment and limited the building of trust and safety. It also stifled candid feedback.

The 2014–2015 Ohio State Buckeyes football team won the College Football National Championship under Coach Urban Meyer by beating Oregon 42–20. Over the course of the season, the Buckeyes were 13–1, only losing to Virginia Tech early in the campaign. Overcoming adversity, the team won the Big Ten Championship, the Sugar Bowl, and the National Championship with its third string quarterback, Cardale Jones. What set the team apart and made them special was its incredibly strong culture.

- Purpose: The OSU Buckeyes purpose was "Nine Units Strong." That motto meant that all nine facets of the team—quarterbacks, running backs, wide receivers, tight ends, offensive linemen, defensive linemen linebackers, cornerbacks and safeties—had to operate at the highest level and in-sync.
- Values: the team's stated values were:
  - Relentless Effort: Go as hard as you can for four to six seconds from Point A to Point B.
  - Competitive Excellence: Constant focus on mental repetitions and physical repetitions.
  - Power of the Unit: Uncommon commitment to each other and to do the work necessary to achieve our purpose.

- Safe, connected, and engaged environment: Coach Meyer created an environment where both players and coaches strove for knowledge and improvement. If there was a better way to do it, everyone was encouraged to speak up.

These are just a few examples of how organizational culture plays a role in a group's success or failure. While your organization is unique, it can draw lessons or ideas from these examples.

BUILDING CULTURE

Culture is never static in an organization. It is always growing or receding. Once you have your purpose, values, and engagement established, it takes hard, intentional work to build culture. There are many ways to encourage growth, but here are the six best that I have seen:

- Lead the conversation: Being intentional and creating the space as a leader to get to know your colleagues and help your team get to know one another helps strengthen connections within your group and promotes your culture. One simple and engaging way to do this is by beginning your next meeting with interesting questions. Here are three questions to use:
    - How did you support the organization's purpose last week?
    - Can you tell a story about how you exhibited one of the organization's values from last week?
    - What is one thing a peer or coworker has done for you since that you really appreciated?
- Regularly revisit the concepts of your culture: Include a slide in your meeting slide deck that summarizes your

organization's culture. Revisit one of the values or behaviors during each weekly or biweekly meeting.
- Make others feel seen and valued: Continue to grow the safe, connected, and engaged environment by showing appreciation and celebrating successes of any size. Look for opportunities to use:
    - Peer recognition. Have a peer recognize another peer's outstanding performance.
    - Handwritten notes. Send a letter (not an email!) to someone who has exceeded expectations.
    - Zoom social get-togethers. Host opportunities for personal interaction to help build the engaged environment.
- Use the AAR after large and small events to discuss, learn, and grow together.
- Use the organization's history to reinforce concepts around the group's purpose and values.
- Revisit the organization's purpose and values annually—doing the *purpose* and *values* exercises every year ensures that the new members understand the values and the values are reinforced with the veterans as your team changes.

The B-17 squadrons of the 8th Air Force used four of these techniques to build their gritty culture. First, their leaders, like Jimmy Doolittle and Curtis LeMay, epitomized the culture, led from the front, and led the conversations about their culture. They used military medals to recognize outstanding members of the team—seventeen aviators earned the Medal of Honor while serving with the "Mighty 8th." Although a new organization, they displayed their brief history in the mission art in the officers' club, the nose art painted on the bombers, and the mission symbols painted on the plane for each successful bombing mission to help tell the story of their culture. Finally, of course, they used the debriefs to connect the crews, build the gritty culture, and make themselves a better organization.

OBSTACLE

One of the toughest challenges in building a gritty culture is mixed messaging, where leaders say one thing but reward another. For instance, if the company says it values its people but promotes a manager who treated his people poorly but got results, it sends a mixed message across the organization. The team is confused. Does the company want results or to treat its people well? Make sure you, as well as your other leaders, are living the values and rewarding the values you say are important. If that isn't happening, it's time to revisit the values and make sure everything is in alignment. Don't send mixed messages.

CONCLUSION

Putting people on the moon, fighting a counterinsurgency in Afghanistan, bombing Nazi Germany, making great movies, and winning national championships all needed gritty organizational cultures that enabled amazing accomplishments. The beliefs, values, and behaviors were different for each of the groups, yet each adhered to their purpose, got the group to understand and live their values, and learned and grew as an organization. Your group may not be pursing manned space flight, but the principles are the same: develop a gritty organizational culture and your team can accomplish the impossible.

Chapter 16

GRITTY TEAM BUILDING

"As I look back on the officers and men who served in Easy Company during the war, my thoughts always return to the corps of soldiers who survived Toccoa ... Toccoa men are special."

Major Dick Winters

NEAR THE VILLAGE OF TOCCOA, in northeast Georgia, is a small, nondescript mountain that towers over the surrounding countryside. The locals called it "Currahee Mountain" after the Cherokee Indian word for "stands alone." Today, the summit is covered with towers, but in 1942, as the United States had just entered World War II against Germany and Japan, it was bare. With the odds stacked against the country, the US Army opened a training camp for paratroopers at the base of the mountain. Nearly 17,000 paratroopers trained at Camp Toccoa during the war. The red clay of Currahee Mountain helped to transform the men from all walks of life from civilians into tough paratroopers.

BAND OF BROTHERS

There were over one thousand infantry companies (an airborne company had about 130 people assigned to it at full strength) that fought in the European theater of operations in World War II. Yet one company is more famous than all the rest: Easy Company (Easy was the word for "E" in the phonetic alphabet), 506th PIR, 101st Airborne Division. By my count, there are at least fifteen books about the company, including the *New York Times* bestselling book *Band of Brothers* by Stephen Ambrose, the HBO miniseries *Band of Brothers*, and a half-dozen documentaries. This exposure has made Easy Company's experience the epitome of the entire generation's experience in World War II.

The 506th PIR was one of the first units in the US Army to take soldiers directly from civilian life, conduct basic training, advanced training, and deploy to combat. The regiment had the ability to select only the best individuals and send the rest who didn't make the cut to other units. During the training at Toccoa, 400 officer volunteers were whittled down to the regiment's 148 best officers. It is estimated that 5,300 enlisted volunteers were tested to find the 1,800 enlisted paratroopers who eventually made up the regiment. Due to their demanding selection criteria and tough training, the 506th PIR and Easy Company were elite organizations.

Tough physical fitness was a critical part of building the team. Each Monday, Wednesday, and Friday, the company would run up and down Currahee Mountain in under fifty minutes. Tuesday, Thursday, and Saturday the paratroopers would tackle the obstacle course. Other physical fitness events included the push-up, pull-ups, rope climbs, broad jumps, road marches (hikes with full equipment), and log exercises. As the soldiers' muscles hardened and endurance grew, the 506th added additional training in infantry tactics, map reading, orienteering, first aid, close order drill, marksmanship, and eventually, mock day and night attacks.

Basic parachute training happened at Toccoa, too. The future paratroopers learned how to conduct a parachute landing fall by jumping off a small platform, exiting a mock airplane, and steering a simulated parachute. Eventually, Easy Company would practice exiting a thirty-four-foot tower, which replicated the initial exit from the aircraft. The officers earned their airborne wings at Toccoa in November, but the enlisted soldiers had to wait to travel to Fort Benning in December to conduct their five parachute jumps.

Toccoa was where the officers and noncommissioned officers of the 506th PIR learned their craft in teaching, training, and leading the paratroopers. The unit weeded out those who didn't meet the high standards, and those soldiers who remained formed incredibly tight bonds between each other. During the paratroopers' time at Toccoa, they formed amazingly tight teams with their bunk and squad mates, forged the culture of the paratroopers and the 506th PIR as they learned to operate independently, earned their airborne wings, adopted the motto "Currahee," and received the right to blouse their boots. Most importantly, they developed the processes at the platoon, company, battalion, and regimental level that they would use to fight and win in combat.

Easy Company, however, had it far from easy under the petty tyranny of Herbert Sobel, the company commander. Sobel's drive and desire to have the best unit in the regiment pushed Easy Company a little farther than the other eight rifle companies in the regiment. Although he had the rank and position, his lack of confidence during field exercises, inability to read maps, bullying, and poor judgment inspired hatred in the men of Easy Company. This shared hardship and shared enemy brought the Easy Company team together. The officers who survived Sobel eventually occupied key positions throughout the 506th, and the soldiers, the Toccoa men, eventually became noncommissioned officers who led Easy Company through some of the toughest times in Normandy, Holland, and Bastogne.

As Stephen Ambrose concludes, Sobel must have been doing something right in the summer of 1942 at Toccoa.

Easy Company was built into a gritty team at Toccoa. Selecting only the best paratroopers, tough physical training, living together, shared meals, and the common enemy of Herbert Sobel forged Easy Company into an exceptionally gritty team, or, in other words, an organization that possesses the "will to persevere to achieve long-term goals." Organizational grit is forged by providing the team a goal and a purpose, a plan, a scoreboard, a gritty culture, and building trust in the team, just like Easy Company.

HIRING

Unlike Easy Company in World War II, you may not be able to hire only volunteers out of the millions of soldiers drafted in the US Army and then take only the top third of that elite group. Although gritty organizations are more than just the sum of the gritty people on the team, there are situations when it is helpful to hire people with gritty backgrounds as a start point.

As part of your hiring process, you may want to try to determine your applicant's grit. It is not worth using a grit quiz, like in Chapter 1, or asking direct, gritty questions because both can be gamed in the interview process. Instead, focus on the applicant's past gritty achievements at work and in life. Here are six questions to consider using during the interview:

- What is your most significant achievement that took the most time to accomplish?
- What achievement did you strive for but fail to accomplish? How long did you pursue it before you gave up?
- In the last twelve months, what long-range goal, either personal or professional, did you achieve?

- In the last twelve months, did you have any personal or professional long-range goals that you worked toward but didn't achieve?
- What was your biggest professional failure? How has that failure influenced you professionally since?
- Did you wrestle, box, or practice martial arts in junior high school, high school, or college?

Once you have an understanding of the applicant's grit, it may be worth looking at them from the perspective of both talent and grit. Some professional sports teams have begun to use a matrix like the one below to differentiate their potential talent. Of course, the best players are in the upper right with high talent and high grit. Riskier players for the teams to pursue are the ones with high talent and low grit or low talent and high grit. Most professional sports teams aren't going to draft, trade, or hire anyone they consider in the low grit and low talent area.

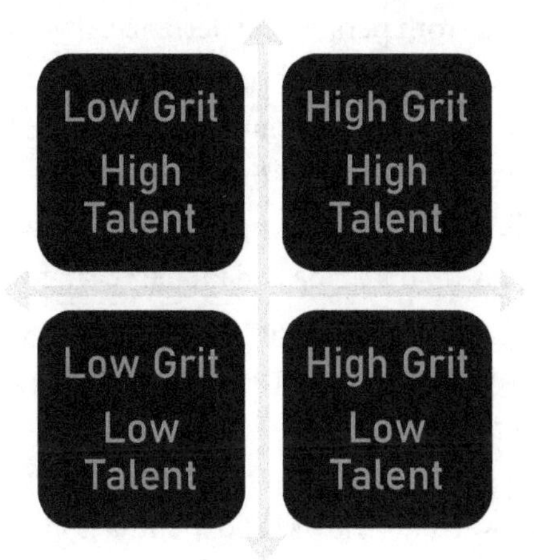

Hiring for Grit

Looking back on my high school athletic career, I fell within the low talent, high grit area. I am still this way today in both cycling and triathlons. Modifying your hiring process so you understand your applicant's grit is a helpful perspective and one which may result in a higher performing team.

TEAM BUILDING

Once your team is set, trust is built in your teams through shared experiences and hardships. Research has shown that team building activities can positively enhance team performance, increase communications, and build trust. The five team building activities that produce the best results are physical activities, field trips, professional development activities, shared meals, and volunteering.

Let's take a deeper look at each of the activities and discuss ideas on how you can use them to build your team.

- Physical Activities: Sports are great ways to bring the team together, get exercise, and see people in a different setting. Speaking from personal experience, if your team is bigger than four people, a golf outing isn't recommended—the foursomes limit the amount of team building that can happen. Ultimate frisbee, ultimate football, flag football, soccer, softball, paintball, ziplining, hiking, whitewater rafting, and even a group bike ride can all help bring groups together.
- Field Trips: A trip to a museum, a sporting event, or a park can bring new ideas to the team and help build the bonds within the team.
- Professional development activities: Workshops, guest speakers, trade shows, and webinars can get your team thinking about new ideas or revisiting the fundamentals of something you do regularly.

- Shared Meals: Rather than everyone eating at their desks, a gathering over lunch is a great way to encourage casual conversation, get to know one another's interests outside of work, and build the bonds within the team.
- Volunteering: An activity the entire team can feel proud about doing can bring it together. A construction project for a good cause or volunteering at a shelter or food bank can help people get to know one another outside of work and build bonds within the team.

The organizations I was part of in the military relied heavily on physical activities, field trips, professional development events, and shared meals to build the team. I can still remember some of the flag football games I played in and the field trips we took over the years, while memories of the PowerPoint-driven meetings have faded away.

VIRTUAL TEAM BUILDING

A virtual team typically describes a group of individuals who work together from different geographic locations and use technology such as emails, texts, Slack, WhatsApp, Microsoft Teams, and Zoom to collaborate. The COVID-19 pandemic created many new virtual teams when the threat of the virus forced more people to work from home. In the future, the cost savings of not having office space may motivate many companies to rely more heavily on virtual teams.

Virtual team building events are valuable too. Good virtual events are challenging to execute; it is helpful to be deliberate and rehearse them before doing them live for the first time. Here are three virtual team building activities that enhance performance, increase communications, and build trust.

- Virtual professional development: Bring in a guest speaker via Zoom or Teams.
- Leader Decision Exercise (LDX): An LDX is a military technique that uses a scenario to give leaders the opportunity to develop a plan based on limited information in a time-constrained environment. Think of them as a situational puzzle, but one not as complicated as a business school case study. LDXs require few resources and provide huge returns in developing your leaders. All it takes is a PowerPoint slide with the scenario and Zoom or Teams to bring the group together for an hour.
- Shared meals: Host a virtual happy hour at 4:00 p.m. on a Friday. It gives your team a chance to end work early and socialize. Plus, you don't have to watch everyone try to eat on Zoom or Teams.

Whatever technique you choose, team building doesn't happen organically, especially in a virtual environment. There has to be time on the calendar each month or quarter to intentionally build your team's bond. Find the time to do one of these events in the next three months.

CORPORATE TEAM BUILDING EXAMPLE: SQUARESPACE

Based in New York City, Squarespace is an American website-construction and hosting company founded in 2004 by Anthony Casalena in his dorm room at the University of Maryland. It has grown into an exceptionally popular website design and hosting platform. With over $500 million in revenue and over 1,000 employees last year, it is regularly voted as one of the best places to work.

Since the company's start, Casalena focused Squarespace on beautiful design. This goal enabled it to gain market share in a crowded market. To support this goal, he hired talent that all "have a similar aesthetic and are wired with a design-focused mindset." I used Squarespace to build my website. I found it easy to use and aesthetically pleasing.

In addition, Casalena has built strong teams in Squarespace using shared experiences and hardships. Samantha Kogle, Squarespace product designer, says, "I like to think of our team as family oriented—we get coffee and lunch together, share inspiration and memes in Slack, celebrate both big and small wins together, and in general, foster a positive environment." Mackenzie Clark, a senior software engineer, highlights the twice-a-year "Hack Week" where engineers have a full week to build whatever they want. It's always a mix of technical explorations, internal products, or new Squarespace features that haven't made it into the road map." These shared experiences, meals, and the "Hack Week" have built strong bonds, great communications, and trust among Squarespace employees. Squarespace is a gritty, high-performing team.

SPORTS TEAM BUILDING EXAMPLE: THE TOUR DE FRANCE

The Tour de France (TDF) is the biggest cycling event in sports. In 2020, twenty-two cycling teams with 176 riders raced during twenty-one stages (a day's worth of racing, usually 100+ miles) over 2,156 miles of French countryside. Each day's race is a separate competition, and the overall race results is a competition as well. Although an individual rider will don the yellow jersey as the overall race winner in Paris, the race is a test of perseverance and the strength of the team.

Each TDF team has eight cyclists under a team director (think coach) with different roles and abilities. There is typically an overall rider (called the General Classification contender), a sprinter specialist, a couple of mountain-climbing specialists, and four all-around helpers called *domestiques* (their job is to do the hard work to get the others into a position to win). Lots of leadership training uses sports as an example. I like the TDF as an example for corporate groups because the bicycle teams have to execute and perform every day for over three weeks. As with corporate groups, building a team to operate at a consistently high level, day in and day out, is more challenging than surging once a week, like in other sports.

Team Ineos Grenadier won the TDF from 2015–2019, so it is useful to look at their team building philosophy. For noncycling fans, Ineos is like the New York Yankees in baseball or the New England Patriots in football—fans either love them or hate them. Team Ineos is a massive organization with the ability to field a team at several cycling races simultaneously. Under the leadership of Sir David Brailsford, the team has a budget of $52 million per year (believed to be more than any other team), thirty riders, and seventy-six team members including sport directors, performance coaches, doctors, psychologists, chefs, mechanics, and brand managers.

Team Ineos Grenadier builds its team very deliberately. The goal of Team Ineos is to win the TDF and as many other bike races as they can. Each year Ineos lays out a roadmap for the season that usually revolves around hiring the best bike racers, hard training, being disciplined, and being dedicated to the pursuit of marginal gains—a series of tiny improvements in many different areas that result in a win. The concept of marginal gains isn't new; it is borrowed from the Japanese concept of *kaizen*, which got global attention in the 1980s. For Ineos, the concept of marginal gains includes a better bus for the riders, an air-conditioned truck for the mechanics, separate washing machines for each rider's kit, biofeedback for each rider, keto nutrition, and much more. The team also develops trust in each other during tough training camps in remote locations, shared meals, and through the rigor of the early season races, like the Criterium du Dauphine and the Tour de Swiss.

Team Ineos Grenadier didn't win the TDF in 2020. Their best rider, Richard Carapez, finished thirteenth. The team later rebounded and won the Giro d'Italia and came in second at the Vuelta a España. Not a typical year for Team Ineos Grenadier, but they still ended up as the third-best team in cycling. Yet their strong team building skills were clearly evident as the team overcame the challenges of the pandemic and achieved success.

OBSTACLE

One of the biggest inhibitors of teamwork is lack of comradery. The normal day-to-day may not build the trust and cohesiveness needed to bring the team together to perform at its grittiest. Using physical activities, field trips, professional development, shared meals, and volunteering events in a deliberate, regular manner can help foster the bonds needed to build a gritty, high-performing team.

CONCLUSION

You may not be developing a team that needs to parachute into Normandy, building the next Squarespace, or training the team to win the next Tour de France, but hiring talented, gritty people and building a better team can produce outstanding results in any organization. The first step in building a gritty team is assembling people who can help the organization grow its grit. Whether building a military unit, a corporate group, or a sports team, leveraging shared experiences and hardships such as physical activities, field trips, professional development, shared meals, and volunteering is the best way to build a team. Great teams don't happen organically; they must be grown. Go on the offensive and enhance your organization's grit by building a gritty team.

Chapter 17

GRITTY LEADERSHIP

"Leaders provide inspiration in a variety of ways—giving energy, particularly at the toughest of times, as that can truly be a force multiplier.... They provide steadfast leadership in the face of adversity. They convey the importance of the tasks in which the organization's members are engaged. They are present at the 'point of decision' during critical moments. They provide an example of fortitude, forthrightness and determination."

General David Petraeus

LEADERSHIP IS THE PROCESS OF influencing people by providing purpose, direction, and motivation. Gritty organizations do not grow organically; leadership is the catalyst. Sam Walton's leadership developed Walmart into a gritty organization and the largest retailer in the world. Howard Schultz's leadership and focus on purpose grew Starbucks into a gritty company that dominated the coffee market. Sara Blakely's grit and perseverance grew Spanx from her apartment into a global brand. Dick Winters' leadership transformed Easy Company into a gritty unit and the best rifle company in the European theater during World War II. Grant's grit at Shiloh snatched victory out of the jaws of defeat. The common denominator in all these gritty groups is their leadership.

Leadership, in the end, means delivering results. Whether it is profit in the corporate environment, fundraising in the nonprofit world, wins in sporting competitions, or victories in battle, leaders must deliver results. Building a gritty organization, or one that possesses "the will to persevere to achieve long-term goals" takes an enormous amount of leadership. Building the grit often doesn't bring about short-term rewards. It takes months and years of dedicated, purposeful leadership every step of the way to provide the team a purpose, communicate a goal and a plan, develop a gritty culture, and build trust in the team.

Leading an organization is tough no matter what the environment. Three ideas can help make it a little simpler and get you the results you want. First, understanding how grit works in you helps you better understand how it works in others. Second, leading by example and modeling the grit you want others to demonstrate is an incredibly powerful tool. And finally, making a conscious decision about using an appropriate leadership style for your people and your situation can inspire groups to move together toward a goal.

GRITTY LEADERSHIP OF YOURSELF

"Know yourself and seek self-improvement" is a US Army leadership saying that applies to all leaders. Leaders like Ulysses S. Grant, Sara Blakely, and Michael Jordan knew that before they could grow grit in their team, they needed to understand and develop their own personal grit. The foundation of gritty leadership is understanding how grit works in yourself and what inspired you in teams and cultures you've been a part of.

Leaders need to know and feel how grit works within themselves. If you skipped Chapters 1 through 9, you may want to go back and read them. Before you can ask others to increase their grit or help develop the organization's goals, you need to know your personal purpose as well as how you persevere, bounce back from defeats, and deal with your fears in the pursuit of your own personal goals.

Another aspect of knowing and leading yourself is reviewing your personal experiences with teams and cultures. Think about the best and worst teams you've been on. What motivated you on the great teams, and what do you never want to replicate from the bad teams? Think about the best and worst organizational cultures you have been part of. Once again, think about what motivated you in the great cultures and what you never want to see again from the worst ones.

Once you understand what works for you as part of a team and as part of a group's culture, it gives you insight into how to lead your group better.

LEAD BY EXAMPLE

As a leader in the US Army, I always tried to lead from the front. The infantry's motto is "Follow Me!" The idea of leaders taking the first step is important on the battlefield, in the board room, and on the playing field.

Once you have mastered your own personal grit, leaders must model the gritty behavior that you want. Want the employees in the store to be friendly to every customer? You need to be friendly with every employee and every customer you interact with every day. Need the team to put in the long hours at practice working on their defense? Be there to turn the lights on, coach them while they are there, and turn the lights off when the last player wants to go home. Want your military unit to be able to march long distances and be ready to fight? Put on your ruck and start walking. In short, lead by example.

The most critical way you lead by example is your decision about where you spend your time as a leader. Where you spend your time tells the group what is important and what you value. For example, if your people are a priority, your organization's leaders must spend time and interact with your people. If you spend all day sending emails and attending meetings with the executive team, it sends the message that perhaps the people in the group are not that important.

Not leading by example sends mixed messages to the team and sabotages your culture and teamwork. For example, one division commander during the surge in Iraq was afraid to go outside the wire. He would never drive anywhere, flew from base to base, and would demand elaborately staged ten-minute walks within sight of the safety of the walls of a FOB as his "combat patrols." His unwillingness to accept the same level of risk for himself, that he asked from the 20,000 people who worked for him, caused resentment in the team, inhibited his impact as a leader, and destroyed trust.

LEADERS GETTING RESULTS

Daniel Goleman is an author and science journalist who has written extensively about the brain and behavior. After surveying 3,000 executives, he found that leaders use one of six leadership styles. These leadership styles aren't personality traits; rather, they are leadership tools to be kept in your leadership toolbox. The six leadership styles are authoritative, coaching, affiliate, democratic, pacesetting, and commanding.

Thoughtful leaders use one, two, or all of the leadership styles in their toolbox to get results, especially to build gritty organizations. The style you select is based on you, your people, and the situation. There is no right answer, but selecting the proper leadership style needs to be a conscious decision. You can't just always default to a commanding style because it is what you are most comfortable with. Repeated use of a style that doesn't fit your people and the situation can do significant damage to the organization.

The Six Leadership Styles

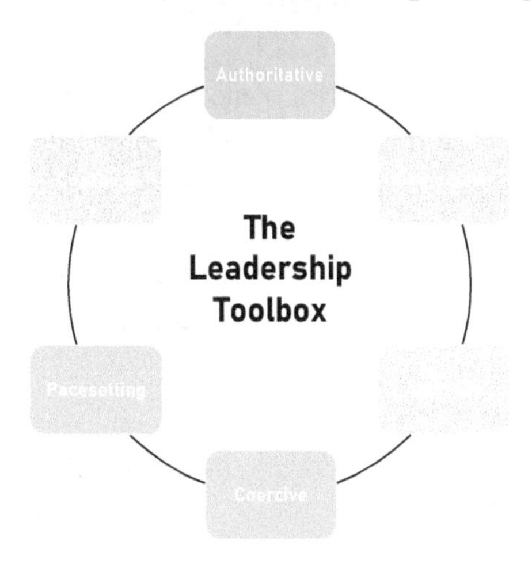

The Six Leadership Styles

The six leadership styles are:

- Authoritative: Mobilizes people toward a vision. This style works best when a clear direction or change is needed and is epitomized by the phrase "Come with me." It helps to create a positive climate.
- Coaching: Develops people for the future. This style works best when helping people and building long-term strength. It is represented by the phrase "Try this." It is part of building a positive climate.

- Affiliative: Creates emotional bonds and harmony. This style works best to heal rifts in teams or motivate people in stressful times. It is epitomized by the phrase "People come first." It helps craft a positive climate.
- Democratic: Builds consensus through participation. This style works best to create consensus or get input and is embodied by the phrase "What do you think?" It helps create a positive climate.
- Pacesetting: Expects excellence and self-direction. This style works best to get quick results from a highly competent team and is captured in the phrase "Do as I do, now." It can create a negative climate.
- Commanding: Demands immediate compliance. This style works best in crisis or with problematic people. "Do what I tell you to do." It can contribute to a negative climate.

Goleman's research also found that leaders who master four or more styles get the best performance out of their group. According to Goleman, the most useful leadership styles to have in your toolbox are the authoritative, democratic, affiliative, and coaching styles.

To continue the toolbox analogy, a leader needs to identify if the group needs you to use some oil, a hammer, or maybe a screwdriver to get the job done effectively and efficiently. As you think through transforming your group into a gritty organization, think about the different leadership styles you may need to use at each stage.

For example, a client who grew her gritty team and increased sales 30 percent in the process used all six styles. First, she used a democratic style to set the purpose and plan. She used pacesetting when she needed to lead by example and make sales calls herself. She also demonstrated the work ethic she wanted the team to use. She then transitioned to using a coaching style to build the team. Finally, she used the affiliative style to develop the culture. Along the way, she had to use a commanding style to put an employee on a three-month performance plan and an authoritative style in the immediate aftermath of discovering a ransomware attack. After six months, she could see the progress in the team—they were much better at handling adversity and were focused on attaining their long-range goal of increasing sales.

In another example, General David Petraeus deployed to Iraq in February 2007 to take over Multi-National Force-Iraq (MNF-I) and lead the coalition forces during the surge. Things looked bleak when he took over, with sectarian violence at all-time highs, Sunni and Shia insurgent groups regularly attacking American forces and fighting with each other, and the destruction of the Shia mosque in Sunni-controlled Samarra the previous year still a source of grievance that resulted in sectarian attacks. The United States committed itself to sending an additional five brigades (about 30,000 troops) to Iraq to reverse the trends. As General Petraeus observed on taking command, the situation was "hard, but not hopeless."

After Petraeus spent a few weeks on the ground in Iraq, he used an authoritative style to get his direct reports out to see the situation on the ground for themselves. He used a democratic style to get all his commanders in the room and agree on the "big ideas" that needed to be pursued going forward—the principles for which had been captured in the Army Field Manual published several months earlier under Petraeus' oversight in the United States. The group embraced four big ideas: first, the human terrain—the people—was the decisive terrain; the people had to be secured, but could only be secured by living with them, establishing bases in their neighborhoods—a 180-degree change from the strategy of the previous two years. Second, the coalition had to clear areas of insurgents and then hold those areas, not clear and hand off or leave. Third, the coalition could not kill or capture its way out of the industrial-strength insurgency it faced; rather, it had to reconcile with as many of the rank-and-file fighters as was possible. And fourth, MNF-I had to pursue the "irreconcilables"—the leaders of the insurgent and militia groups—even more relentlessly than it had before. As the force began implementing the four big ideas, he used a coaching style with the division commanders to ensure that they understood what he wanted and were moving out to accomplish it. He used a combination of authoritative and pace-setting styles with the commanders who lagged. At regular intervals he brought the team back in, listened, took feedback, and communicated a common picture of the situation. He coached the commanders to share lessons learned, and constantly sought to ensure that the Multi-National Force was a learning organization. All of this took a combination of authoritative and democratic approaches. The strategy worked—violence was driven down significantly across Iraq, by 85 percent in the course of the eighteen months of the surge. In summary, General David Petraeus used a variety of leadership styles to lead MNF-I, get results, and increase the safety and security of Iraq and the Iraqi people.

OBSTACLE

Once you understand yourself, lead by example, and decide on what Leadership styles work with your group, the biggest obstacle in growing a gritty organization is deciding what aspects of leadership and the team need emphasis and which ones can be ignored. Experience, intuition, and a bias toward action must guide you. For example, a corporate group might need a better plan and a renewed emphasis on culture but less time on teamwork. A sports team might need to refine its purpose, find players with more grit to help with the culture, and spend less time on its plan that worked well last year. Finally, a nonprofit might need to develop a scoreboard and work on its teamwork while spending little time on its well-understood purpose. There is no single, correct answer, but making a decision and leading your organization toward developing its grit is always better than doing nothing.

CONCLUSION

Leading a team is never easy. There is no magic bullet for developing and leading a gritty organization. Understanding how you personally get gritty is the first step, leading by example is the second step, and consciously using the right leadership style to bring out the best in your people in a given situation is paramount. Keeping these three ideas in mind as you grow grit in your bicycle team, your small business, or your military unit can make the leadership journey an extraordinary one.

Chapter 18

ORGANIZATIONAL GRIT BLUEPRINT

"It takes as much energy to wish as it does to plan."

Eleanor Roosevelt

WISHING YOUR GROUP HAD ORGANIZATIONAL grit won't make it happen. Providing the team leadership, putting together a plan, and executing the plan is the only way grit grows. The last seven chapters have covered a lot of ground on how to build and maintain your organization's grit, or "the group's will to persevere to achieve long-term goals." Leading your group, defining your organization's purpose, crafting a leader's intent, establishing goals, building plans, enhancing your culture, and building your team are all tough tasks each in themselves.

What is Organizational Grit?

The group's will to persevere to achieve long term goals

Organizational Grit

Eleanor Roosevelt was the First Lady of the United States of America and the United States Delegate to the United Nations General Assembly for five years. Also, she was a talented writer, speaker, activist, and organizer who advocated for civil rights for African Americans and greater equality for women. As she remarked, "In the long run, we shape our lives, and we shape ourselves. The process never ends until we die. And the choices we make are ultimately our own responsibility." Roosevelt made the personal choice to use her leadership skills to grow organizational grit in the UN and the Presidential Commission on the Status of Women. But she might have been able to grow even more grit and accomplish greater achievements if she'd had a blueprint for how to grow organizational grit.

BLUEPRINT

The word *blueprint* used to refer to an engineering drawing used in construction. Because the technique of producing blueprints is obsolete, a blueprint is now used to describe any type of plan. To help reduce some of the uncertainty, use this blueprint below to help build your organization's grit. Feel free to modify it or use it as is.

The expression "building the plane while in flight" has become increasingly common in business, sports, and the military. The phrase captures the thoughts of risk and uncertainty that come with designing new concepts and testing them in real time with actual participants, all while being responsible for keeping existing operations running. It reflects the idea that you need to try to build something different, even as you still have your employees, players, or soldiers on board the plane. The risky, uncertain aspects of growing your grit while maintaining current operations feel all the more critical under the unrelenting pressure of a board of directors, shareholders, fans, politicians, the press, or the public.

The challenges in creating an exceptional organization are complex and do not lend themselves to clear-cut, one-and-done solutions. They require a complicated transformation of systems, cultures, and beliefs, and grit is only one system among many. Transforming systems and processes means simultaneously creating plans, designing strategies, and implementing them, all while leading the group, troubleshooting problems, and making midcourse adjustments. It isn't easy by any stretch of the imagination.

The most important aspect of the blueprint is not the creation of the organization's purpose, leader's intent, plan, culture, or teams. Instead, the time spent leading, communicating to, listening to, and learning from the organization and its stakeholders is more critical—I call this the *pause and communicate* step. Back to our plane analogy, there are steps in the blueprint where you pause and communicate to buy time and space for the leader and the team so if the wings aren't working quite right, the plane can continue gliding along until everything gets adjusted based on what was learned. Equally important is to make sure you, as a leader, are comfortable with owning and sharing this learning with the team and stakeholders.

Stop wishing, and use this blueprint as a way to increase your confidence in your azimuth as you navigate your organization to a destination with greater purpose, culture, and grit. Use it to enhance the support for your journey from the team and its stakeholders. Use it to decrease some of the uncertainty and avoid the same mistakes as others who have gone before you. Finally, use it to enable you to reach your target swiftly, all while building a gritty organization while in flight.

GROW YOUR ORGANIZATIONAL GRIT BLUEPRINT

- ☐ Lead your team. Set a gritty example, listen, and communicate.
- ☐ Survey your organization to get an idea of how gritty it is. Use the questions in Chapter 11 to help develop your perspective on the organization.
- ☐ Pause, listen, and communicate. Listen to the feedback you get and continue to refine your perspective. Talk to the leaders, the team, and your stakeholders about how you view your current level of organizational grit.
- ☐ Develop (or review) your organizational purpose. Use the exercise in Chapter 12 as a way to start the conversation.
- ☐ Pause, listen, and communicate. Listen to the feedback you receive on your purpose and continue to improve it. Talk to the leaders, the team, and your stakeholders about your organizational purpose.

- ☐ Develop (or review) your leader's intent and the leader's intent of your direct reports. Use the exercise in Chapter 13 as a way to get everyone to produce a rough draft of their leader's intent.
- ☐ Build your goals and your annual plan to reach them. If you have a planning process already in place, use it. If not, try the technique described in Chapter 14.
- ☐ Pause, listen, and communicate, communicate, communicate the goals and the plan to your leaders, the team, and stakeholders. Listen to the feedback you receive so you can make the goals and plan even better.
- ☐ Review your organizational purpose and then develop (or review) your organizational values. Use the exercise in Chapter 15 as a catalyst.
- ☐ Pause, listen, and communicate your organization's purpose and values to the team and stakeholders. Listen to the feedback you receive so you can make the purpose and values even better.
- ☐ Select monthly or quarterly activities that create shared experiences or shared hardships and will have the greatest impact at building your gritty team. Utilize Chapter 16 for ideas. Ensure that these events happen regularly and are incorporated into the plan.
- ☐ Provide leadership to the team.
- ☐ Monthly
    - Goal/Plan: Take stock of where you were, what you've accomplished so far, where you are, and where you are going. Then ask, is it still the right goal?
    - Communicate your understanding to the team and stakeholders so everyone has the same picture. Listen to the feedback to improve your understanding and your azimuth.

- ☐ Quarterly
  - Goal/Plan: Take stock of where you were, what you've accomplished so far, where you are, and where you are going. Then ask, is it still the right goal?
  - After Action Review: If there was a success or a failure during the quarter, ensure you have conducted an AAR (see Chapter 15) to make sure you and the group understand what went right and what needs to be improved next time.
  - Culture: Assess where you and your team are at living the organization's values and what needs to be improved.
  - Team Building: Ask yourself and your team the following questions: Do we need to hire a gritty individual? Are the team building activities building or diminishing the connections in the organization? What can be done better?
  - Communicate your understanding to the team and stakeholders so everyone has the same picture. Listen to the feedback to improve your understanding.

If you reach your goal, pause, celebrate, and communicate the success to your team and its stakeholders. Host an AAR (see Chapter 15) to capture what went right and what needs to be improved next time. Then go back to the top and start a new, grittier journey.

If you don't reach your goal in twelve months, go back to the top and reexamine the grit in your organization, your purpose, your leader's intent, your goal, and your plan. If the goal is still relevant, host an AAR (see Chapter 15) to capture what went right and what needs to be improved next time. Revise your plans. If the goal is not relevant, start over and apply what you have learned to a new gritty journey.

Chapter 19

CONCLUSION

"First, forget inspiration. Habit is more dependable. Habit will sustain you, whether you are inspired or not ... Habit is persistence in practice."
Octavia Butler, author

OCTAVIA BUTLER WAS AN AMERICAN science fiction writer who received a MacArthur Fellowship, two Hugo Awards, and two Nebula Awards. After watching a bad science fiction movie as a nine-year-old, she realized that she could write a better story and get paid for it. From high school through her late twenties, she often woke up at two or three in the morning to get some writing done before heading to her shift at the factory. During her career, she always wanted to "tell stories filled with facts. Make people touch and taste and know. Make people feel!" Her most popular books are *Kindred, Parable of a Sower* and *Parable of the Talents.*

One of Butler's themes in *Parable of a Sower* is that you can't stop change, but you can shape it. Grit is in the same category. It is always growing or declining within yourself and within groups. You can't stop the everchanging grit, but you can shape it in yourself, others, and in the organizations that you lead. No one has ever said it is easy, though.

FORWARD OPERATING BASE ANDAR, GHAZNI, AFGHANISTAN, NOVEMBER 21, 2010

I started out with a story from Afghanistan, so I thought another would help wrap things up. On a slow-moving Sunday in November, I had just sat up in my bed in a tent on FOB Andar. There was a chill in the air as I pulled on my top and started tying my boots. I thought to myself that if we were back in the States, we would be getting ready to watch a pro football game.

Suddenly, there was a shriek and a huge explosion directly behind my head. My ears rang and my head throbbed. The concussion kicked up dust from the floor and turned the inside of the tent into a fog. I grabbed my hat and ran out of the tent. Smoke was curling up from the top of the HESCO barrier, a wire cage that held dirt and gravel, fifteen feet behind my tent. I walked around the HESCO wall and saw that the impact was near the top. "Another couple of feet higher and it would have landed in my tent," I thought to myself.

I started checking on the soldiers around me. We were lucky that day—no one was hurt. The Taliban had tried to send a message with a 107mm rocket, just like the ones we found in the grove of trees months before.

The sun went down that night and the war kept grinding on, just as it did for the nine years before and another decade after we left. We attacked the Taliban. The Taliban attacked us in an endless cycle of violence. I turned and walked toward the headquarters. In spite of the attack, there were more important things to do. I needed to make sure the battalion continued to pursue our leader's intent, maintained our culture, and developed the bonds in the team. Our gritty organization, the Iron Rakkasans, would keep fighting in Afghanistan, trying to make a difference until the last soldier was on a plane home to Kentucky.

FINAL THOUGHTS

Reading this book may have been persistence in practice for some of you. For me, writing the book was a gritty journey. I started out writing a few blog posts on grit. Then, like Octavia Butler, the habit of writing every day took hold and revealed the path to an entire book. I wrote chapters out of order. I wrote whole chapters only to delete them as I revised the book. I wrote and rewrote sections. Other people provided comments and ideas. I rewrote chapters again. As many authors have experienced, putting this book together was a long and winding journey. I know this book won't win me a MacArthur Fellowship, but I hope the facts resonated, your senses were stimulated, and you felt better equipped to grow your grit.

I want you to remember some of the inspiration in this book. I want you to remember the stories of John D. Rockefeller, Amelia Earhart, Sara Blakely, Dan Gable, and Misty Copeland as they used their purpose to organize the oil industry, push boundaries with their goal setting, persevere to scale a company from an apartment, rebound from defeat, and manage their fear of failure. I especially want you to be inspired to go after your goal by using the tips in the book to discover your personal purpose, develop your perseverance, enhance your resilience, fuel your motivation, and cultivate your grit.

I want you to remember the stories of Walmart, Starbucks, small groups of paratroopers on D-Day, NASA during the Apollo program, and Easy Company, as well as their efforts to develop into gritty organizations that created great companies, helped the Allies achieve victory in World War II, put a human on the moon, and overcome incredible odds at Bastogne. I particularly want you to be inspired by the techniques that help you develop an organization's purpose, construct a plan, develop a gritty culture, and build a team. Without energetic and determined leadership, it's impossible to grow an organization's grit and accomplish amazing things.

Yet, it's not enough to just read and think about your grit. Take This book, re-read the chapters, underline the passages that motivate you, make notes, and develop a plan to build your personal or your organization's grit—or both! If you are lost on where to start, use the checklist in Chapter 10 to energize growing your personal grit or use the grit blueprint in Chapter 18 to grow your organization's grit.

There are fifty-two weeks in a year. Every week contains 168 hours. Every day there are 1,440 minutes. Every second, every minute, every hour, every day, and every year counts. There is never a perfect time to start growing your personal or organization's grit, but you have to start somewhere. And like the old adage goes, "There is no better time than the present." You've read the book. Now it's time to get to work and grow your grit.

For more information on how you can grow your grit, I encourage you to visit my website at www.thefivecoatconsultinggroup.com Or contact me directly at david.fivecoat@thefivecoatconsultinggroup.com. On the website, I offer more articles and tools that you can use to gain greater insight into and development of your grit. If you really enjoyed the book, please leave a review on Amazon or Goodreads.

NOTES

Introduction

For more on Paktika Province and 3rd Battalion, 187 Infantry's counterinsurgency operations there, see Wesley Morgan's "Fighting Hard and Soft Counterinsurgency on Holy Ground," *The New York Times*, July 8, 2010 and "Elusive Game in Afghanistan," *The New York Times*, July 14, 2010, as well as Ward Carroll's "A Tough Road Ahead for Afghan Governance," *Military.com*, May 17, 2010.

For more on grit, see Angela Duckworth's *Grit: The Power of Passion and Perseverance* (New York: Scribner, 2016), Paul Schultz's *GRIT: The New Science of What It Takes to Persevere*, Flourish, and Succeed (Climb Strong Press, 2014), Shannon Huffman Polson's *The Grit Factor: Courage, Resilience, and Leadership in the Most Male-Dominated Organization in the World* (Harvard Business Review Press: Boston, 2020), Logan Strout's *The Grit Factor: 15 Attributes to Doing Life Better* (New York: Morgan James Publishing, 2021), and Darrin Donnelly's *Old School Grit: Times May Change But the Rules for Success Never Do* (Columbia, SC: Shamrock Media, 2016).

Chapter 1: Personal Grit

The story on Ulysses S. Grant at Shiloh is from Ron Chernow's *Grant* (New York: Penguin Press, 2017). For more on Ulysses S. Grant and his amazing grit, see Ulysses S. Grant's *Personal Memoirs of U. S. Grant* (New York: Da Capo Press, 1982). The New Year's resolution statistics came from Dan Diamond's "Just 8% of People Achieve Their New Year's Resolutions. Here's How They Do It," *Forbes Magazine*, January 1, 2013. For more on willpower and some of the science behind grit, read Kelly McGonigal's *The Willpower Instinct* (New York: Avery, 2012). For more on the average American in 2018, see Phillip Bump's "This is What the Average American Looks Like in 2018," *The Washington Post*, August 13, 2018.

Chapter 2: Find Your Personal Purpose

The best book on John D. Rockefeller is Ron Chernow's *Titan: The Life of John D. Rockefeller, Sr.* (New York: Vintage Book, 1998). Simon Sinek's *Start With Why* (New York: Penguin Group, 2009) helped me with my personal purpose. The four other books to inspire your personal purpose are: David McCullough's *The Wright Brothers* (New York: Simon and Schuster, 2015), Margot Lee Shetterly's *Hidden Figures* (New York: William Morrow, 2016), Jon Krakauer's *Into Thin Air* (New York: Villard, 1997), and Gayle Tzemach Lemmon's *Ashley's War: The Untold Story of a Team of Women Soldiers on the Special Operations Battlefield* (New York: Harper Collins, 2015).

Chapter 3: Improve Your Goal Setting

For more on Amelia Earhart, see Candace Fleming's *Amelia Lost: The Life and Disappearance of Amelia Earhart*, New York: Schwartz & Wade, 2011) and Jerry Alder's "Will the Search for Amelia Earhart Ever End?" *Smithsonian Magazine*, January 2015.

To know more about Gene Kranz and Apollo 13, I recommend Gene Kranz's *Failure Is Not an Option: Mission Control from Mercury to Apollo 13 and Beyond* (New York: Simon and Schuster, 2000).

Chapter 4: Enhance Your Perseverance

For more on Sara Blakely, see Charlie Wetzel's *The Spanx Story: What's Underneath the Incredible Success of Sara Blakely's Billion Dollar Empire* (New York: Harper Colins Leadership, 2020) and Claire O'Connor's "Undercover Billionaire: Sara Blakely Joins the Rich List Thanks to Spanx," *Forbes*, May 7, 2012. Jim Collins's *Good to Great* (New York: Harper Collins, 2001) does a marvelous job with the flywheel and momentum.

Chapter 5: Develop Your Resilience

For more on Dan Gable, Dan Gable's *A Wrestling Life: The Inspiring Stories of Dan Gable* (Iowa City, IA: University of Iowa Press, 2015) is a good place to start. Also, John Irving's "Gorgeous Dan," *Esquire*, April 1973 is fun to read. For more on sleep, fitness, and nutrition, read *O2X Human Performance's Human Performance for Tactical Athletes* (Tulsa, OK: Fire Engineering Books, 2019), Dan John's *Never Let Go: A Philosophy of Lifting, Living, and Learning* (Santa Cruz, CA: On Target Publications, 2009), Jack Groppel's *The Corporate Athlete* (New York: John Wiley and Sons, 2000), Jim Loehr and Tony Schwatrz's *The Power of Full Engagement* (New York: The Free Press, 2003). For more on mindfulness, read Dan Harris's *10% Happier* (New York: It Books, 2014).

Chapter 6: Forge Stronger Courage

Rivka Galchen's "An Unlikely Ballerina: The Rise of Misty Copeland," *The New Yorker*, September 15, 2014 and Misty

Copeland's *Life in Motion: An Unlikely Ballerina* (New York: Simon and Schuster, 2014) Are enjoyable to read. Yoda is quoted from Matthew Stover's book *Star Wars: The Revenge of the Sith* (New York: Del Ray, 2005). Tim Ferris's *The 4-Hour Workweek: Escape 9–5, Live Anywhere, and Join the New Rich* (New York: Crowne Archetype, 2009) introduced the idea of listing your fears.

Chapter 7: Upgrade Your Motivation

There are several books on Michael Jordan. I like David Halberstam's *Playing for Keeps: Michael Jordan and the World He Made* (New York: Random House, 1999.) The ESPN/Netflix documentary *The Last Dance* was very insightful as well. Daniel Pink's Drive: *TheSurprising Truth About What Motivates Us* (New York: Riverhead Books, 2009) is a great place to start to understand drive and motivation.

Chapter 8: The Mundanity of Grit

For more on Justice Ruth Bader Ginsburg, please see Irin Carmon and Shana Knizhnik's *Notorious RBG: The Life and Times of Ruth Bader Ginsburg* (New York: Harper Collins, 2015) and Ruth Bader Ginsburg's *My Own Words* (New York: Simon and Schuster, 2016). Daniel F. Chambliss's "The Mundanity of Excellence: An Ethnographic Report on the Stratification and Olympic Swimmers" in *Sociological Theory*, Spring 1989 sparked my ideas on grit being mundane and a habit. For more on habits, see Charles Duhigg's *The Power of Habit: Why We Do What We Do In Life and Business* (New York: Random House, 2014), James Clear's *Atomic Habits: An Easy and Proven Way to Build Good Habits and Break Bad Ones* (Penguin Random House, 2018), and Gretchen Rubin's *Better Than Before: Mastering the Habits of Our Everyday Lives* (New York:

Crown Publishers, 2015). Finally, Andy Weir's *The Martian* (New York: Broadway Books, 2014) is a fantastic book and movie.

Chapter 9: Grit Crucible—US Army's Ranger School

More on Colonel Tex Turner can be found in Chapter 4 of Ivan Prashker's *Duty, Honor, Vietnam: Twelve Men of West Point Tell Their Stories* (New York: Warner Brothers, 1988). A recent article on the challenges of Ranger School is Will Bardenwerper's excellent "Army Ranger School Is a Laboratory of Human Endurance" *Outside Magazine,* April 20, 2020. Also, Chapter 6 in Rick Atkinson's *The Long Grey Line* (Boston: Houghton Mifflin Company, 1989) does a fantastic job describing Ranger School. Finally, more on Kristen Griest is in Dan Lamothe's article "Female Soldiers Provide Their First Account of Completing Ranger School," *The Washington Post,* August 20, 2015.

Chapter 10: Personal Grit Checklist

Mia Hamm's *Go for the Goal: A Champion's Guide to Winning in Soccer and Life* (New York: Harper Collins, 1999) gives more insight into Mia and her incredible career. For more on checklists, see Atul Gawande's *The Checklist Manifesto: How to Get Things Right* (New York: Metropolitan Books, 2009).

Chapter 11: Organizational Grit

Walmart's story is told through Sam Walton's *Sam Walton: Made in America* (New York: Bantam Books, 1992) and Charles Fishman's *The Wal-Mart Effect* (New York: Penguin Press, 2006). The statistics on long-term companies came from an article by Dominic Barton, James Manyika, Tim Koller, Robert Palter, Jonathan Godsall, and Josh Zoffer,

"Where Companies with a Long-Term View Outperform Their Peers," *McKinsey Global Institute*, February 8, 2017. Dunham's number is covered by Malcolm Gladwell in his book *Tipping Point: How Little Things Can Make a Big Difference* (New York: Little Brown and Company, 2002). Thomas Lee and Angela Duckworth's "Organizational Grit," *HBR Magazine*, September-October 2018, provided a useful perspective.

Chapter 12: Cultivate Your Organization's Purpose

Howard Schultz's *Onward: How Starbucks Fought for Its Life without Losing Its Soul* (New York: Rodale Books, 2011) helped me with the Starbucks story. Eliza Green's "Finding Your Why: A Brand Purpose Exercise," www.oliveandcompany.com/blog/finding-your-why December 12, 2018 was enlightening as well.

Chapter 13: Develop Your Leader's Intent

Guy Lofaro's *The Sword of St.Michael: The 82nd Airborne Division in World War II* (Philadelphia: Da Capo Press, 2011) is a great book on the All-Americans in World War II. Current Army doctrine on the commander's intent is found in *ADP 6-0, Mission Command: Command and Control of Army Forces* (Washington, DC: HQ Department of the Army, 2019). Chad Storlie's "Manage Uncertainty with Commander's Intent," *HBR Magazine*, November 2010, gave me another perspective on the commander's intent. Finally, Gary Hamel and C. K. Prahalad's "Strategic Intent," *HBR Magazine*, July-August 2005, provided other ideas.

Chapter 14: Basic Planning

Dwight Eisenhower's *Crusade in Europe* (New York: Da Capo Press, 1977), Alan Axelrod's *Eisenhower on Leadership* (San Francisco:

Jossey-Bass, 2006) and Susan Eisenhower's *How Ike Led: The Principles Behind Eisenhower's Biggest Decisions* (New York: Thomas Dunne Books, 2020) helped me understand General Dwight D. Eisenhower. Jocko Willink's *Extreme Ownership: How US Navy SEALs Lead and Win* (New York: St. Martin's Press, 2015) helped me sort through my ideas on military planning and apply them to the corporate environment.

Chapter 15: The Culture of Grit

For more on NASA during the Apollo program, see James Donovan's *Shoot for the Moon: The Space Race and the Extraordinary Voyage of Apollo 11* (New York: Hachette Book Group, 2019), Andrew Chaikin's *A Man on the Moon* (New York: Penguin Group, 1994), and Nancy Atkinson's *Eight Years to the Moon* (Salem, MA: Page Street Publishing, 2019). I found Daniel Coyle's *The Culture Code* (New York: Bantam Books, 2018) very helpful. For more on the 8th Air Force and the B-17 bomber pilots, see Donald Miller's *Masters of the Air* (New York: Simon and Schuster, 2006), Warren Kozak's *Curtis LeMay: Strategist and Tactician* (Washington, DC: Regnery History, 2009) and John T. Correll's article "The Real Twelve O'clock High," *Air Force Magazine*, January 1, 2011. Ed Catamull's *Creativity, Inc.: Overcoming the Unseen Forces that Stand in the Way of True Inspiration* (New York: Random House, 2014) has great ideas about emulating Pixar's culture. Finally, the Ohio State Buckeye football example is from Urban Meyer's *Above the Line: Lessons in Leadership and Life from a Championship Season* (New York: Penguin Press, 2015).

Chapter 16: Gritty Team Building

For more on Easy Company, please see Stephen Ambrose's *Band of Brothers: E Company, 506th Regiment, 101st Airborne Division from*

Normandy to Hitler's Eagle's Nest (New York: Touchstone, 1992), Dalton Einhorn's *From Toccoa to the Eagle's Nest: Discoveries in the Bootsteps of the Band of Brothers* (BookSurge Publishing, 2009), and Dick Winters' *Beyond Band of Brothers: The War Memoirs of Major Dick Winters* (New York: The Berkley Publishing Group, 2006). Patrick Lencioni's *The Five Dysfunctions of a Team: A Leadership Fable* (San Francisco: Jossey-Bass, 2002) and Stan McChrystal's *Team of Teams: New Rules of Engagement for a Complex World* (New York: Portfolio, 2015) influenced my ideas on team building.

CHAPTER 17: GRITTY LEADERSHIP

Two articles informed this: Daniel Goldman's "Leadership that Gets Results," *HBR Magazine* March-April 2000 and General David Petraeus's editorial "Five 'Big Ideas' to Guide Us in the Long War," *The Washington Post*, April 25, 2016.

CHAPTER 18: ORGANIZATIONAL GRIT BLUEPRINT

The best biography of Eleanor Roosevelt's amazing life is David Michaelis's *Eleanor* (New York: Simon and Schuster, 2020). This chapter also draws on the ideas from Atul Gawande's *The Checklist Manifesto: How to Get Things Right* (New York: Metropolitan Books, 2009).

CHAPTER 19: CONCLUSION

Octavia Butler's *Parable of the Sower* (New York: Grand Central Publishing, 1993) is an incredible book

INDEX

Page references for figures are italicized.

ABOUT THE AUTHOR

For the past four years, David G. Fivecoat has helped enhance the leadership of hundreds of individuals and improved the processes of dozens of companies on battlefields and in workshops as the founder and managing partner for The Fivecoat Consulting Group (TFCG). He blogs, speaks, coaches gritty leaders, and helps develop gritty organizations.

Previously Colonel Fivecoat served twenty-four years as an infantry officer. He led men and women during contingency operations in Kosovo and Bosnia, three combat tours in Iraq, and a combat tour commanding a battalion in Afghanistan—over forty-one months in combat. He culminated his service by overseeing the gender integration of the US Army's Ranger School.

David earned a bachelor of science in Military History from the United States Military Academy, a Master of Military Arts and Science from the US Army Command and General Staff College, and a Master in National Security Strategy from the National War College. He was the lead writer for the US Army's *Field Manual 3-24.2, Tactics in Counterinsurgency*, as well as numerous articles.

David's military decorations include the Valorous Unit Award, four Bronze Star Medals, the Army Commendation Medal with V Device, the Ranger Tab, the Master Parachutist Badge, and the Combat Infantryman's Badge. He is a Distinguished Member of the Airborne and Ranger Training Brigade.

In his free time, David skis, competes in triathlons, and is an avid bicyclist. He resides in Columbus, Georgia, with his daughter.

You can follow him at www.thefivecoatconsultinggroup.com.

CPSIA information can be obtained
at www.ICGtesting.com
Printed in the USA
JSHW041642250721
17214JS00002B/10

9 781736 893319